I Became What I Wanted To Be

Lewis Cedar

I Became What I Wanted To Be

The Songs Of Lewis Cedar

Lulach Publishing

I Became What I Wanted To Be
The Songs Of Lewis Cedar

Copyright © Lewis Cedar and Lulach Publications 2024

The right of Lewis Cedar to be identified as author of this work has been asserted in accordance with the Copyright, Designs and Patents Act 1988. Many characters and events described in this book are fictional and any resemblance to actual persons, living or dead, is purely coincidental.

Published by Lulach Publishing 2024

https://www.lulachpublishing.com

All rights reserved. Except for the quotation of short passages for the purposes of criticism and review, no part of this publication may be reproduced, stored in a retrieval system, or transmitted, in any form or by any means, electronic, mechanical, photocopying, recording or otherwise, without the prior permission of the publisher.

Lewis Cedar
I Became What I Wanted To Be

British Library cataloguing in Publication Data. A Catalogue record for this book is available from the British Library.

ISBN 978-1-7396723-9-3

BISAC MUS000000   MUS017000   MUS052000

Typeset in Elatan

Second Edition 2026

I Became What I Wanted To Be

One Hundred and Fifteen Songs By Page Numbers

Across The South China Sea 44
Anke's Song 70
As Far As Hong Kong 94
A Set Of Magic Tricks 234
Back In The States Said The GI 58
Bad Boy 189
Bananas 124
Chain Of Freedom 190
Chewee Chewee Chewing Gum 202
Ching Chong China Man 118
Chocolate Milk 192
Christine's Smiling Like The Sun In June 113
Christmas Night 210
Councillor Chedwiggen 154
Did You Hear About The Man Who Lost His Trousers 132
Did You Hear The Spanish Lady 100
Did You Ever Have A Dream 232
Dream Dream Dream 103
Elephant Parrot and Kangaroo 194
Elm Fires 16
Enjoy The Itch Don't Scratch It 156
Experience 47
Fight The Tide 162
Game Boy 122
Go To Singapore 198
Granddad's Car Horn 197
Hangs Together 82
He Gave Her The Frangipanni 78
He Just Wanted To Fly 200
Hedgehogs 204
Hey Holly 162
His Gazoo 226
Hong Kong Monsoon 206
Hotel In Germany 20
I Bought You To The Alpine Mountains 50
I Can 126

I Could Say That I Miss Annie 88
I Hope That The Years and You Have Been Good Together 104
I Hope You Will Remember This Song 155
I Say You're Beautiful 178
I Was Born Here 110
I Wish You Had Have Come Along 32
I'd Love To Know 27
If I Could Be What I Want To Be 236
If I Had Done Something Else 60
If You Thought That The Rails Were Forever 160
I'm The Boy Who Played Tom Paxton's Guitar 106
It's Funny How People Can Be 128
It's Just The Being With You 144
Juke Box Baby 68
Jungles of Borneo 208
Just Nice Words 36
Just To Survive 57
Kalamansi 48
King Fisher 186
King Ludwig 213
Knight At Your Round Table 174
Land of The Filipino's 98
Lean On Me Any Time That You Want Too 66
Lovely Weather 30
Man With One Shoe 182
Marry Me 164
Marvellous Restaurant 18
Maybe If I Want Too 31
My Your Life Be An Apple Crumble 165
Mister Producer Make Me A Star 92
Mombassa 42
Mrs Beckham 116
My Passport Says Planet Earth 90
Nairobi 40
Nigel's Song 72
Oh You Have A Lovely Voice 158
Old Grey Coat 22
Oo Char Tr La La 120
Ozone Layer 230
Peter Pan Summer 52

I Became What I Wanted To Be   7

Photographs 24
Plus Est En Vous – More Is In You 136
Pyjama Game 188
Rainbows 214
Rapunzel Let Down Your Hair 150
Rattattattooee 212
Relax Baby Life's A Choice 148
Richmond Lullaby 81
Routes De Soleil 185
Say You Can 152
She Powers What I Can Be 102
Sing It One More Time Again 172
Spanish Dancer 37
Wake Up In Your House 168
Sweet Years 77
Tavernelle 28
The Berlin Zoo Song 217
The Forth Bridge Song 170
The Gift To Be Free 114
The Highway Man 176
The Policeman's Find 222
The Portuguese 224
The Swedish Reindeer Song 220
The Traveller 180
Three Pretty Ladies 166
Time 134
Time To Start Out On Your Own 108
Uncle Percy 130
Up In The Clouds 228
Victory Is Ours 54
Water 218
We Went To Vienna 74
What About Our Baby 49
What Did Mrs Beatie Do 62
What Do You Do In Holland 38
What I Want To Be 236
When I'm 63 146
When I Was Your Age 86
When The Lady Says Goodbye 84
Your New Song 34

Introduction Page 9
Index Page 240

I Became What I Wanted To Be

In 1974 I wrote a song I called 'If I Could Be What I Want To Be'. I had been going about the Folk Clubs writing wee songs and I wanted to make a career in the business of entertaining people. I thought I could find nice gentle people who would listen to my simple melodies and that they would give me money so I could live. I had visions of making records and them sending me into the record charts.

I knew nothing of course, although I had already learned much. The Folk Clubs were a good place to learn, indeed they were full of tolerant people who turned a deaf ear to un-tuned guitars and singers who had little experience. They were also places where one could see the musicians who were good and the ones who got paid for their efforts. I earned money at the weekends so that I could I travel to folk clubs on as many nights of the week as I could and tried to get 'floor spots'. This was an unpaid opportunity to sing, usually, three songs.

Some of the people who were going about at that time were: Bully Wee, Cliff Aungier, Diz Disley, Joe Stead, Hamish Imlach, Johnny Silvo, June Tabor, Raggy Farmer, Isla St Clair, Pete Atkin, Noel Murphy, Wizz Jones, Richard Thompson and Linda Peters, Gryphon, Dick Gaughan, Derek Brimstone, Jeremy Taylor, Mike Maran, Gordon Giltrap, Frogmorton, Marianne Segal, Ralph McTell, Christie Hennessy, Jasper Carrot, Roger Williamson. Nigel Cameron, Dri

Jinja. All of these extraordinary people inspired and pushed me along. Some became best friends and some helped in the most wonderful ways.

I got my name into the 'Melody Maker' and the 'New Musical Express'. I ran my own club and I became resident singer at one of the biggest clubs.

From there I took the leap into pub singing, a very different beast, where proper money was paid and, what some considered 'proper' entertainment, was expected. The first proper paid gig was Hogmanay 1973 into 1974 my pal Mervin Hall and I got away with it, we were praised and then paid. The following Hogmanay I was on my own in a fierce pub in north London things did not go well. After my first song a man came up and shouted at me 'CAN YOU SING ROCK A ROUND THE CLOCK ?' I said no he said 'WELL WHY DON'T YOU F...K OFF THEN.'

I survived. I made a diary of success and failure, I noted what was good and what was bad. After one of the early shows a man said to me you sing and play guitar really well. The problem is you sing all the wrong songs. He gave me a list and that list, fifty years later, is still valid in care-homes where people of that vintage now stay.

So from 1974 to 2024 I built a career that took me to Scotland, England, Wales, France, Germany, Belgium,

I Became What I Wanted To Be

Luxembourg, The Netherlands, Switzerland, Austria, Spain, Italy, Cyprus, Kenya, Hong Kong, Singapore, Indonesia, Malaysia, Denmark, Norway, Brunei, Philippines, (*Berlin, Sicily, Penang, Isle of Wight, Harris, Lewis)* For eleven summer seasons I had my own show in one of the great theatres. I performed on radio and television, I acted in television shows. I gave 13584 professional shows until 12 March 2020 when the world went into lock down and Covid ruined much. Since then I have done 22 professional shows and I have made a lot of films. I wrote stories and scripts for plays. There have been records, cassette tapes, CDs and books. I worked alongside some of the most well known entertainers, musicians and managers of my time...

Labi Sifre, Helen Shaprio, Kenny Woodman, David Whitfield, Johnny Spillers, David McWilliams, Len Tucker, Danny La Rue, Norman Newell, Bob Kember, Kenny Woodman, Bride Reid, Norman Vaughan. Dave Arnold, Iris Williams, Eddie Francis, Oliver Reed, Richard James, Barry Vines, Melvin Hayes, Wendy Padbury, Richard O'Sullivan, Tony Britton, Molly Studron, Ian Lavender, Donald Hewett, Peter Egan, Keith Barron, Nigel Davenport, Kenny Everett, Average White Band, John Castle, Michael Palin, Cheryl Campbell, Tim Piggot Smith, Denholm Elliot, Michael Kitchen, David Troughton, Jenny Agutter, Jeremy Kemp, Gloria Huniford, Tommy Vance, Adrian Love, Geoff Love, Judy Geeson, Martin Jarvis, Max

Wall, Gordon Kaye, Sam Waterson, David Suchet, Ed Bishop, Peggy Ashcroft, Lional Jeffries, Peter Chelson, Shelagh McLeod, Martin Shaw, Bob Smyth, Robert Lindsay, Richard Vaughnan, Michael Crawford, Trevor Eve, Warren Clarke, Dick Emery, Patrick Troughton, Don Estel, Brian Murphy, Roy Kinnear, James Bolan, Susan Jameson, David Yip, Susannah York, James Fox, Jane Asher, Peggy Ashcroft, Lionel Jeffries, Vaughn Savage, Nick Bailey, Tony Banes, Peter Davidson, Benny Hill, The Bachelors, Lena Zavoroni, Lady Elizabeth Anson, David Bedford, John Duncanson, Del Mandel. This list is not comprehensive sorry if I did not put your name down.

Some of the above our paths just crossed on some show or another others became close friends and colleagues.

Then there would be the list of all the wonderful people who gave me work and all those fine people who were my audiences. Thanks to those who did not enjoy my shows and thanks to those who were kind enough to praise and applaud what I offered. I did shows for young and old, all colours and all creeds. For those of sound and not sound mental faculties or physical abilities. Fifty years is a lot to cram into a few paragraphs.

During those years I made many records and I wrote many songs. Some for young people some for adults. I

I Became What I Wanted To Be

made ten professional albums I think. This book is a collection of one hundred and fifteen songs of the many which I have written. Some have not survived the test of time. Some were written for special events which have come and gone. A few of these songs are of me or mine most are simply songs for you to attach your own meanings.

I wrote and had published I think ten books. I under pen names which saved me from typecasting and allowed freedom to transfer from one medium to another without the baggage of what I had previously done.

In the beginning I realised that managers and record companies wanted me for the money they thought they could make from the meagre talents I possess. I also understood that I was not much of a team player, I like to work things out myself and I like to do everything, I like variety. Some I knew spent time fawning after record contracts. I went hunting for audiences. The greatest thrill to this day is to confront a bunch of strangers where my challenge is to get them on my side and give them an enjoyable time from the entertainments I present. Most people have a yard stick based upon fame and fortune. I had my full of fame very quickly.

Working television was sitting about for ages to do a wee bit that flashed on and off the screen so quickly I wondered why it took so much time to produce.

I owned a big house and new cars and endured some horrid experiences personally. What I will never regret is finding my own way and making my own business in a totally different way from many of my contemporaries who are now forced to make endless TV travel shows or end up hosting inane TV quizzes and commercials to maintain their celebrity status.

Fame in the modern era is to be shunned. I made a decision that I could spend much of my time competing against my peers or find roads less travelled, as M. Scott Peck wrote. I have spent a life achieving professionally -'Being What I Want To Be' - So being what I wanted to be. I am not fond of the cabals and groups people form. I never wasted time competing with others on the greasy fame an fortune pole. In many ways I have been less successful in my personal life but I did what I could, sorry if I was not good enough.

I would wish that you can be what you want to be. I think it is more difficult to do that in these times than when I started out.

Elm Fires

The embers of the old elm logs are sleeping

the somnolent fire leaves the air cre-ee-eping

with the scent of ash and wood

wanting the day that will be so full of meaning

the day I can say this is the only way-ay-ay

the day that I'm singing for you

the sound will be grand and all according to plan

and we will know that it's good

and we will know that it's good

MSCP/PRS 323492LQ ISWC: T-011.458.310-6 Written in 1974

I Became What I Wanted To Be

I visited folk clubs every night of the week that I could. I often missed the last bus and ended up walking and walking and walking home. There where many Elm trees that had suffered Dutch Elm Disease and these were felled and burned I walked passed the smouldering embers of many of these poor trees.
This song was looking forward to the career I was planning to make.

By Kim Traynor - Own work, CC BY-SA 3.0, https://commons.wikimedia.org/w/index.php?curid=17372763

Marvellous Restaurant

I'm afraid that the butter is rancid
the milk is sour the meats in transit
potato's are burned the sugar is solid
cup of tea is cold-old
-o-l-l-ed

I'm afraid that bread is mildew
tomato's are black and the cocoa's like stew
fridge is broken the kettles got a hole in
coffee's damp with the morning dew-
oo-oo-i-oo-oo

and I'm afraid that the waitress is off sick
the cook is old and the pans aren't non-stick
crockery's chipped and the prices have risen
washing up is ready for you-oo-oo-i-oo-oo

I'm afraid that the walls are falling the
windows are dirty
the rent man's calling
cat died after yesterdays mutton
boy have we got food for you-
oo-oo-i-oo-oo

MSCP/PRS 323492LT ISWC: T-011.458.310-6 Written in 1973

I used this for my Opportunity Knocks and first summer season auditions. It lasts just over 30 seconds. I wanted to be different and make a mark. I did. It was unusual and got peoples attention.

I Became What I Wanted To Be

19

Hotel In Germany

```
C                        C
```
There was an old hotel in Germany
```
F                        F
```
but I can't quite remember that song
```
G7                  G7
```
all about a lonely guy
```
G7                             C
```
who hadn't seen his girl for so long

it was a cold night in autumn
```
F            F
```
he was feeling blue
```
G7                        G7
```
and although I felt sorry for him
```
G7                     C
```
I was glad he had not met you
```
F          C          C
```
*if he had he'd have cried and cried
```
F          C
```
cried himself to sleep

We were supposed to stay in an old German farm house. Kitchen to the right, living room to the left and above the bedrooms. Under the bedrooms between the kitchen and living room were the farm animals, who 'in former times' (German friends often used this expression) would have been an integral component of the house heating system. In amongst their accommodation was the lavatory. It had a wall around it about a metre high so when in use the donkey could observe all the user was doing and in my experience it would voice it's approval or maybe dismay. I had an allergic reaction to the animals so I had to go to an hotel.

        F   C
      knowing that you were so far away
        G7   G7
      and your arms were out of reach
                C
      now I'm in this cold hotel in Germany
            F   F
         finding it hard to sleep
G7   C
laying here thinking of you with every breath I breath

    it's a cloudy night and the wind has changed
          F   F
      but it hasn't brought you to me
       G7   G7
     I'm thinking about that young man
       G7   C
   and I know if he'd met you he'd agree

MSCP/PRS 323492LS ISWC: T-011.458.310-6 Written 6 September 1978

> The hotel was an old fashioned place. I was on my first visit to Germany and wondered what ghosts were lurking. I found interesting things in the supermarket., things not available at home, cherry juice and lovely yoghurt. I wrote this song in the hotel room. I was thinking about the Harvey Andrew's song 'Friends of Mine', I saw him I think at the Hendon Folk Club once. He sang his 'Soldier' Song that night. I also saw the great Jake Thackray at Hendon. I filmed with the BBC in Hendon, the 'Secret Army', looking back Hendon was quite a big part of my career. (The picture is of the house and the Donkey)

Old Grey Coat

G Em G Em G Em
G   Em
Take off that old grey coat my love
G   Em
put a blue one on for me
G   Em
smile with your own green eyes
G   Em
smile and let me see

Am   D7
*smile and let me see
        G
for you're beautiful
Em
when still and calm
Am   D7
and when you touch me

G   Em
take off that old brown coat my love
G   Em
put a clear one on for me
G   Em
smile with your own clear eyes
G   Em
smile and let me see

*
G   Em
I don't remember your rough tongue my love
G   Em
when you speak softly to me
G   Em
take me with your soft warm breath
G   Em
smile and let me see

I used this along the Marvellous Restaurant for Opportunity Knocks audition. On first listening it is the last word which reveals what it is all about. I wanted to be different and make a mark. I did. It was unusual in intrigued. I wrote it in Swanage Durlston Bay

G   Em
I've known you when your rough
G   Em
I've seen you when your calm
G   Em   G
I've know you wild and free
Am   D7   G
but now you're soft oh sparkling sea

Photographs

```
    C                      F             G7
Photographs negatives and smiles of you the album is finished
                       C
             now that we are through
                                F
   the flash gun went bang and the colours all turned blue
      G7                          F          C
       leaving a blurred picture in my memories of

       C              F              G7
  it seems that our love became over exposed to much love light
                       C
            to let the camera man reload
            C                     F
  and the Polaroid camera didn't give an instant end it
       G7                          F          C
       took so long to develop it left time to pretend

    G7                              C
*that our love could be much more than a film that's out of date
    G7                                E7
    you get rose coloured prints but for good results you're too late

       C                            F
       I must have seen it coming but the camera does not lie
           G7                    C
            and there's your picture at the end of July
                                          F
there's a smudge on the print where it was touched before it dried
              G7                F         C
            so that's where it ended that's where it died
```

*

I Became What I Wanted To Be   25

```
         C                      F              G7
I wish I'd kept my thumb over the lens or left it out of focus
                    C
          because now that we're not friends
                              F              G7
the memories would eventually yellow and fade but these
         G7                    F      C
          photographs are forever my memories aid

    G7                              C
could our love could be much more than a film that's out of date
    G7                         C
      you get rose coloured prints or slides that are second rate
E7                          Am              E7
all the prints are blurred at the edges for good results your to late

         C          F           G7
 all these years later the digital age images shared in an instant
                    C
              up to your web page
 C                          F
       four hundred million pixels wiz around the world
             G7       F         C
          cached forever in a memory swirl
```

MSCP/PRS 323492LV ISWC: T-011.458.310-6 Written in 1979

Tommy Vance

By Ssaco - Own work, CC BY-SA 3.0,
https://commons.wikimedia.org/w/index.php?curid=16436642

This is one of the songs that helped me to gain membership of the PRS-MCPS. In order to become a member one had to have had songs on a record or broadcast on radio or television. I did a radio show with Tommy Vance who praised the song by saying 'clever lyric' or something like that

Photography has changed so much. Now we have no need for films and developing and albums. Nearly everyone has a phone that can take photographs. When I wrote this I owned a Polaroid camera which in those times was MAGIC you could take a picture then pull the film from the camera through metal rollers which pressed a chemical cocktail over photographic paper within a minute or two the photo would appear on the paper. No taking the film to the chemist shop and them sending off to the laboratory and waiting a week for the results. There were lots of things that could go wrong when taking a photograph. Thumbs covering the lens, old film stock could produce pink coloured prints, keeping the camera still was a challenge it was easy to get blurred pictures. Flash guns/blubs provided a very bright light like lightening as a picture was taken the blubs were generally blue. It was easy to over expose a picture with too much light. After a few years prints could yellow and the colour could fade. I added the final verse around 2008 when web pages became the rage.

I Became What I Wanted To Be   27

I'd Love To Know

```
         C                      F
   Little girl over there tell me what are you smiling for
 G7                    C                         CMaj7
why are you so happy  did you like the sound of the chord
         C                    F
   and little boy over there why is your smile so wide
         G7                            C
come on over here and tell me in me you can confide

            F        C    F         C
      *I'd love to know oh tell me tell me what it is
      F              C         G7
   tell me why are you laughing it must be a magic trick

         C                     F
    is it the Christmas coming or is it your Birthday past
 G7                          C
something that will last forever  something that will go by fast
                        F
    is it the sound in the air  is it the smell of the breeze
      G7                            C
   is it the colour of the green leaves  growing on all the trees
                            *

         C                     F
     now I understand you I can see the light in your eyes
         G7                        C
    I can understand your laughter  I know why you smile
                            F
      so take a hold of her hand boy  Treat each other well
      G7                           C
   I can see how much you love him  and I know he loves you as well
                            *
```

MSCP/PRS 323492LR ISWC: T-011.458.310-6 Written 10 September 1978

Tavernelle

```
   G                        Em            C                 D
We drank Chianti with senior Beagi in Tavannelle in old Italy
              D              G
        and the sun shone down
                        Em
          the sun shone down


              Em     C         D
         *in that old Italian town
                    G
      the love went round and round and round
              Em        Em
       the sun shone down and down and down
     Em              C             C     D
      the love went round and round and round

                         *
     G             Em              C                D
he had siesta with a signorina he could not resist her she gave him her pizza
              D              G
        and the sun shone down
                        Em
          the sun shone down
```

Tavernelle Italy

I met Richard James when I was entertaining patients in a Mental Hospital. He had a marionette puppet theatre. He asked me if I would tour Germany with him. That leap lead me around the world. Richard also arranged 'Town Twinning' we drove to Italy to try a twin with Tavernelle

```
        C              G              C              G
    then signor Beagi banged his fist on the table
            C                           D
    he shock all the glasses but his stance was not stable
            C                   D
        he staggered sat down and shouted
                     D
               PREGO……


        G                       Em       C                    D
in the evening there was dancing much romancing and lots of singing
            D               G           Em
       and the sun went down the sun went down
                    Em      C           D
              in that old Italian town
                            G
         the love went round and round and round
            G         Em                    Em
         the sun went down and down and down
    Em              C                       D
       the love went round and round and round
```

MSCP/PRS 323492LW ISWC: T-011.458.310-6 Written in 1979

Lovely Weather

I'd take you to see the flowers
in the April breeze
you'd love to see the water
that gushes from the trees
it's clear so very clear
meandering and free
you* d love to see the flowers
in the April Breeze
I'd take you to see the willow
the ducks upon the pond
I know you'd climb the bridge then
run to the fields beyond
they're green so very green
the grass is very long
you'd love to see the willow
and the ducks upon the pond

MSCP/PRS 323493AP ISWC: T-011.458.310-6 Written 23 April 1974

I Became What I Wanted To Be

Maybe If I Want Too

   CMaj7
    May be if I want too
   Am
    maybe if I can
F   CMaj7
maybe if I have the time I will

   CMaj7
    could be if you will
   Am
    could be if I'm still
F   CMaj7
hanging around perhaps I will

   CMaj7
    wait and see I would
   Am
    and that might happen
F   CMaj7
and if it does we can cry again

    G7   Am
perhaps I will perhaps I will

   CMaj7
    if we miss this one
   Am
    we'll catch the next one
F   CMaj7
if it comes around again

    G7   Am
perhaps I will perhaps I won't
    G7   Am
perhaps I can perhaps I won't float

MSCP/PRS 323493AN   ISWC: T-011.458.310-6 Written 1 July 1974

I Wish You Had Have Come Along

Using the

Dm chord shape on the 5th fret and the 3rd fret pluck the guitar strings 4/2/3/1 using thumb index thumb middle

F#m   F#m
We arrived at Lake Geneva
Em   Em
through the mountains

we passed Dijon
Em7   A7
all the colours were misty
D   D
how I wished you'd come along

because I can't describe the landscape
Em7   Em7
I can't describe the trees
A7   Am7   D
and I can't tell you all the sights and places that I've been

Lac Léman–Lake Geneva–Genf
Richard James and Doug

```
     F#m                        F#m
the cleanness of the water shores
       Em                   Em
     after dirty Paris sun
              Em7
     the smell and taste
              A7
     of the evening air
       D                    D
     how I wished you'd have come

because you can only guess at the colours
       Em7                    Em7
     you can only guess the trees
  A7                     Am7              D
and you can only guess at the sails in the setting sun
```

MSCP/PRS 323493AM ISWC: T-011.458.310-6 Written in 1979

Your New Song

```
     G                       D         C  G
There's nothing like the sea for romanticizing
            F            G
        nothing like the sea
     G                    D    C          G
there's nothing like a breeze on a summers evening
             F            G
        to keep you close to me
     Am                       Em
    there's nothing like the sun in the morning
     Am                Em
      to see your beautiful face
     G                         F
     I'll tell you this and again babe
     F                         G
      it's the best of the human race
       G                   D     C     G
    there's nothing like the birds on a misty morning
              F            G
        For lovers to wake up to
     G              D    C    G
    there's nothing like the seagulls voices
             F            G
        to get you humming too
     Am                        Em
    there's nothing like a stormy evening
     Am              Em
      to keep you by the fire
```

Berwick upon Tweed

       G   F
to see you smile baby
    F   G
no drug could get me higher

 G   D   C   G
there's nothing like the sun to keep me smiling
        F   G
when I can't see you
G   D   C   G   F   G
if the rain falls you'll find me hiding I'll be missing you
Am   Em
there's nothing like the rough cold sea
   Am   Em
to get me wanting you
     G   F
I'll tell you this again
    F   G
you're my only girl I am true

MSCP/PRS 323493AR ISWC: T-011.458.310-6 Written in 1975

Just Nice Words

   C   G7   F   C
Snow gently falling a voice gently
      G7   C
calling now is the right time
  C   G7   F   C
deep rich and fine the dark burgundy
     G7   C
wine warming colour sweet
  C   G7   F   C
sparkling silver-blue ornamented
    G7   C
gold with love for you
  C   G7   F   C
choir boys in rich dark robes starched in white
     G7   C
but borrowed clothes
  C   G7   F   C
lights gently calling thoughts gently warming
     G7   C
across the room
  C   G7   F
blonde hair that sparkles like gold
  C   G7   C
as it tumbles through the air
  C   G7   F
blue eyes that sparkle like soft glow
   C   G7   C
light through a window

MSCP/PRS 323493AQ ISWC: T-011.458.310-6
Written 12 December 1971

I Became What I Wanted To Be

37

Spanish Dancer

G
It was the hip hop hap of the Spanish Dancer
C   G
the clattering castanets guitars were twanging
                                   C   G
maracas were shaking and so was Paul Violet
            Em
because his mother in law was as big as a door
                    G   D   G
and she was about to slam in his face
      Em   C
she was mad as a bull who with the matador was full
              D   G
and Paul was in disgrace

G
one night on a hill his car engine stood still
  C   D   G
in other words the car broke down
                                Em
he walked five kilometre's for a mechanic
  C   D   G
when he returned his wife could not be found

Em   G   Em   G
was she kidnapped by the fairies did the sand man take her away
  C   Em
oh no not at all she went to the local Parador

and she danced the night away

MCPS/PRS Tune Code 323493BN ISWC: T-011.458.310-6 Written in 1986

What Do You Do In Holland

  C   F   F
What do you do in Holland on a cold October day
G7   C   C
when the leaves are turning golden and the sky is grey

when the wind is blowing through the trees
                        F
and you see your breath on the air
             G7
you're glad your not in Amsterdam
F   F   C
but you wish you were with her

    F   G7
because she fills the day so sweetly
C   C   Am
you've got a feeling she always will
G7   C
you know she'll be your lover from now until
    F   G7
she came into your life and altered your plans
   C   Am
and soon she'll come along
G7   C Am
you've got a feeling that this is only her first song

```
C                                F                              F
```
what do you do in Germany when the sun has turned the sky blue
```
  G7                             C                              C
```
the frost has melted on the flowers and made it look like dew

```
              and you would like to share these things
                        F              F
                the river and the bird song
                        G7             G7
                  but she's away in Utrecht
                  F     F                      C
                you could be in Hong Kong
        F              G7             C              Am
```
Luxembourg was beautiful but you wanted to go home to her

MCPS/PRS Tune Code 323493AS ISWC: T-011.458.310-6 Written in 1981

Nairobi

```
     C                      F                  C
*Nairobi Nairobi pick pockets and thieves
     C                 G7                 C
Nairobi Nairobi purple Jacaranda trees
     C                      F                  C
Nairobi Nairobi green city in the sun
     C                 G7                      C
Nairobi Nairobi clouds when the day is done


        G7              C             G7                      C
   you're stuck on top of the world Jomo Kennyatta land
 G7          C                             G7                              G7
half man half god who knows he was Kenya's most powerful man

                                    *

        G7    C                 G7              C
   you came from the railway built on a swamp
 G7          C                                                G7
you can see those bygone days in Nairobi when ever you want

                                    *
```

Nairobi

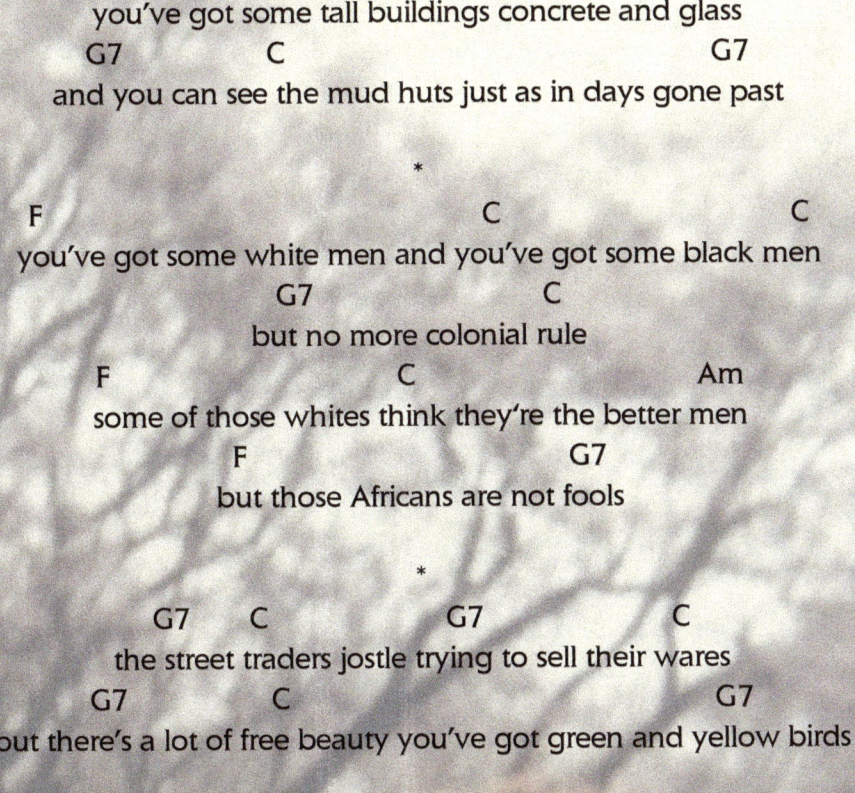

```
      G7    C                G7          C
   you've got some tall buildings concrete and glass
     G7         C                          G7
   and you can see the mud huts just as in days gone past

                            *

     F                       C                       C
   you've got some white men and you've got some black men
                    G7              C
                   but no more colonial rule
     F              C                      Am
   some of those whites think they're the better men
                    F                G7
                but those Africans are not fools

                            *

       G7    C             G7             C
    the street traders jostle trying to sell their wares
     G7         C                                G7
   but there's a lot of free beauty you've got green and yellow birds
```

MCPS/PRS Tune Code 323493AT ISWC: T-011.458.310-6 Written in 1981

Mombassa

Use the D shape chord on the first fret so it is Eb and slide it up to D twice as an introduction

followed by this chord sequence D6 DMaj7 Em7 A7 Am7 C

```
     C                  G          D              D
   Some day I'm going to sail the Indian Ocean with you
 C                      G            D              D
 we'll take a boat from Mombassa and spend a year or two
     C              G          Bb          A
   the sea will be so warm and the sky will be so blue
   D           C                         D
  I'll look into your eyes and I know what we will do


       C             G                      D
   we'll cruise around the islands and see the Philippines
       C              G           D            D
    have tea with Orientals and Christmas on a beach
     C               G              Bb            A
  with golden sun for riches and clothed in the sky
           D            C                     D
         you and I will be lovers in paradise
```

Shelly Beach

```
     C            G             D              D
we'd sail all the way to  China and head for Borneo too
     C            G         D             D
  the trade winds will take us all the way through
       C          G           Bb        A
     we'd live on Pawpaw and Pineapples too
  D                C                           D
and drink fresh passion juice and I know what else we'd do.
  G                   A                       A
we'd make love on the sand in a hundred different lands
                     C       D
                    Ooooooo
```

MCPS/PRS Tune Code 323493AU ISWC: T-011.458.310-6 Written November 1981

Across The South China Sea

```
            F              G7          C           Am
     I'd like to take you back again across the South China Sea
         F            G7           F          G7            F     G7
  buy you some pearls to wear  buy you some silk to wear buy you some flowers to wear
                          C                 Am
                  that would be my Asian dream
             F            G7              C             Am
       but here I am in Hong Kong again missing you every hour
         F              G7           F           G7           F        G7
  I bought you some pearls to wear, bought you some silk to wear only wish that you were here
                        C                Am
                to wear the flowers in your hair
           F          G7          C    F     G7                   C
     don't like being on my own in China life isn't bright when I'm not with you
                        F                         F
            take all the lights from Hong Kong harbour
  C                         Am          F    G7          C    Am
  string them to the moon and a little further life isn't bright when I'm not with you.


                      F            G7   C           Am
              then I'd take you to the west again to old Singapore
         F          G7          F           G7              F            G7
  we could see the Raffles hotel see a new skyscraper as well we could go out on the town
                          C                Am
                  there's plenty besides to do
             F          G7                C              Am
       but here I am in the Sea View hotel where the aircon cools the tropical night
   F          G7       F             G7                F                    G7
  I've seen the Raffles hotel I'm in this new skyscraper as well didn't bother to go out on the town
                        C                Am
                well what's the fun without you
          F    G7       C     F       G7                         C
      here I am in Malaysia where the peoples faces have just got to be seen
                          F                    F
                the sun is warm and the rain is too
   C              Am                    F       G7                 C    Am
  you can keep your hotels and your high living too I'm not living till I'm back with you
```

Beach in Brunei

```
          F           G7         C            Am
       then I'd take you to Borneo the oil state of Brunei
       F          G7              F          G7
       We could see a jungle or two we could see the houses on stilts
                      F               G7
              see the mosque with the golden dome
                    C              Am
              It's religion when I'm with you
   F          G7         C        F         G7         G7           C
but here I am way out in no where this tropical beech is deserted but for me
      F         G7           F         G7      F          G7
I've seen a jungle or two seen the water buffalo too they're building another mosque
                      C             Am
              If you're not Muslim there's nothing to do
       F         G7           C     F   G7  G7           C
       here I am the place is deserted it's a lovely beach but no telephone
                    F                            F
              I could take all the shells and corral Islands
           C             Am    F       G7          C
           make them all your possessions If you where only here with me


              F          G7        C           Am
           then I'd take you away again to the Philippines
   F         G7        F         G7          F          G7
we could take a Jeepnee down we could take a tricycle down we could take a taxi down
                       C              Am
               to some place besides a beech
          F          G7             C         Am
       here I am in Manila harbour where the sunset's just got to be seen
  F         G7          F          G7            F           G7
I've taken a Jeepnee down I've taken the Love Bus down take a 747 down
                    C            Am
              meet me on the beech
       F        G7         C        F    G7                C
here I am with the business men of metro If I gave them your smile they sell it to the world
                    F                    F
              wrap it all up in little red boxes
    C Am            Am       F      G7                C Am
    it would solve their economic crisis I'm having a crisis while I'm not with you
```

Lewis Cedar

              F   G7   C   Am
       Then I'd take you to Borneo the oil state Brunei
F   G7   F   G7   F   G7
We could see a jungle or two see the house on stilts See the mosque with the golden dome
               C   Am
        it's religion when I'm with you
      F   G7   C   F G7   C   Am
but here I am way out in no where this tropical beech is deserted but for me
    F   G7   F   G7   F   G7
I've seen a jungle or two seen the water buffalo too They're building another mosque
            C   Am
    If you're not Muslim there's nothing to do
  F   G7   C   F   G7   C
Here I am the place is deserted it's a lovely beech but no telephone
        F   F
    Take all the shells and coral islands
 C   Am   F   G7   C
make them all your possessions if you were only here with me

MCPS/PRS Tune Code 323493AV   ISWC: T-011.458.310-6 Written in 1983

I Became What I Wanted To Be

Experience

Thank your lord for the experience
all the pictures running through my brain
thank your Lord for the experience
it left me thoroughly drained

all the people went and came
and no one returned in shame

can you live with the experience
now you know things have been tamed
can you live the experience
or has it left you framed

get a hold of the experience
it can leave you with no blame
get a hold of the experience
it cannot return a claim

MCPS/PRS 323493CP ISWC: T-011.458.310-6 Written 1973

Kalamansi

[C] I can bring you back the photographs and tell you where I've [G7] been [G7]
but I can't bring you the flowers the sunshine or the [C] wind
I can tell you of the sunsets and of the rainy [G7] nights
but I can't bring you the surf or the tropical [F] star [C] light

[F] had enough of the South China [F] seas
[C] had enough of the Kalamansi. [C]
[G7] it's been good but it's time to come home to [C] you
[F] had enough of the coconut [F] trees
[C] had enough of strange fishes from the [C] seas
[G7] it's been good but it's time to come home to [C] you

[C] I can bring you lots of souvenirs and tell you the foods I've had to [G7] eat [G7]
but I can't bring you the sweet smells or the far east savoury [C] meats
I can tell you of the drinks I've had to cool the heat of the [G7] day
but the flavours would not been the same with those beaches so [F] far a[C]way

MCPS/PRS Tune Code 323493AW ISWC: T-011.458.310-6 Written in 1983

By Obsidian Soul - Own work, CC0, https://commons.wikimedia.org/w/index.php?curid=81931708

I Became What I Wanted To Be

What About Our Baby

```
     Am                             G
So it finally happened and you're going to go
     F                E7
if you had asked me I would have said no
     Am                 G
and what about our baby he needs us both
       F              E7
now come on lady this is no joke

       F       G7       C      Am
*how can you leave on a sunny day
       F       G7       C      Am   F Am  F Am,
middle of March but it could be May
```

                    *

```
     Am                       G
in the middle of the morning in the middle of the night
       F          E7
you get so angry when I refuse to fight
     Am                       G
but I know my son will learn by what is done
       F              E7
and I want so much to fill his life with fun
```

                    *

```
     Am                 G
you light a cigarette but that won't change things
       F              E7
remember how you smiled at our wedding rings
     Am                     G
I think it's best you leave now I can't stand the smoke
       F              E7
then you will be free to laugh at the joke
```

                    *

MCPS/PRS Tune Code 323493BP ISWC: T-011.458.310-6 Written in 1986

I Bought You To The Alpine Mountains

    C
I brought you to the Alpine mountains
     G7
    what did you say to me ?
                        C
you said that you would rather live by the sea
               G7
so I bought you a house down along the shore

    oh what a mistake that was
       F   C
because now you say it's a bore

  F   C
*so I'm leaving to go my own way
    G7   C
I'm leaving baby it's today
        F   C
because in your eyes all I do is wrong
     G7
and if you had your way
              C
you'd be writing my song

No matter what one does for people some people can never be satisfied a song for most of my romances

Alpine Mountains

I Became What I Wanted To Be

      C
I went to the Philippines
   G7
to get a pineapple
                      C
you screamed for papaya you started to rattle
                            G7
I gave you the pawpaw and you wanted a melon

oh when you are near
     F   C
I could pray indeed for heaven

              *

C
I took you to the South of France
 G7
to Nice and to Cannes
               C
you said it would be Monaco if I were a real man
                 G7
so we went to a hotel by the Casino
                           F   C
and as soon as we got there you said it was time to go

             *

MCPS/PRS Tune Code 323493BM ISWC: T-011.458.310-6 Written in 1986

Casino Monaco

Peter Pan Summer

```
   C                              F
It was a Peter Pan summer  Ianto was dressed in green
   G7                                     C
   Sebastian played Captain Hook  Violetta was Wendy
                                 F
   Toby played Jimmy Cork Screw  Leo was Mr Smee
G7                            F                  C
oh what a summer that was the summer he was three

         F           C       G7            C
   *what a summer that was  what a summer we had
         F           C       G7            Am
      sometimes it was crazy  sometimes it was mad

   C                              F
it was a green and leafy summer when Maggie played Tinkerbell
      G7                          C
   we didn't know if we were in heaven or in hell
                                 F
   we kept right on smiling  all through the summer rain
   G7                            F              C
then it was the autumn and we were back on the road again
```

*

\[Am\] when the pirates came upon us and told us to walk the \[Dm\] plank
\[G7\] some drew their cutlasses but \[E7\] Peter
\[Am\] pulled the plug from the boat that was how it sank

\[C\] it was a bright and sunny Easter the \[F\] crocodiles had gone away
\[G7\] and everywhere there were children \[C\] coming out to play
the time was marching on school was coming so \[F\] was May
\[G7\] and then it would be summer a \[F\] year to the \[C\] day

*

MCPS/PRS Tune Code 323493BQ ISWC: T-011.458.310-6 Written in 1988

By Francis Donkin Bedford - Illustration from "Peter and Wendy" by James Matthew Barrie, Published 1911 by C. Scribner's Sons, New York, Public Domain, https://commons.wikimedia.org/w/index.php?curid=147924058

Victory is Ours

G Em G Em
G   Em
Victory is ours cried the Brigadier
G   Em
my men have fought long they've been without fear
    C   D   G   Em
they battled hard against the enemy
C   D
everyone's proud in the old country
G   Em
the eyes look up as the flag is raised
G   Em
Port Stanley is ours we are quite amazed
C   D   G   Em
artillery lit the long cold nights
C   D
Argentineans gave one hell of a fight

G   Em
victory is yours cried the Falklander's
G   Em
have a drink boys it is all on us
C   D   G   Em
hope you won't mind us making a fuss
C   D
but we're glad you came to rescue us
G   Em
the eyes look straight over Bluff Cove
G   Em
Sir Galahad still burning again she explodes
C   D   G   Em
some blame the Argies some blame the French
C   D
some blame the UN or the lack of defense

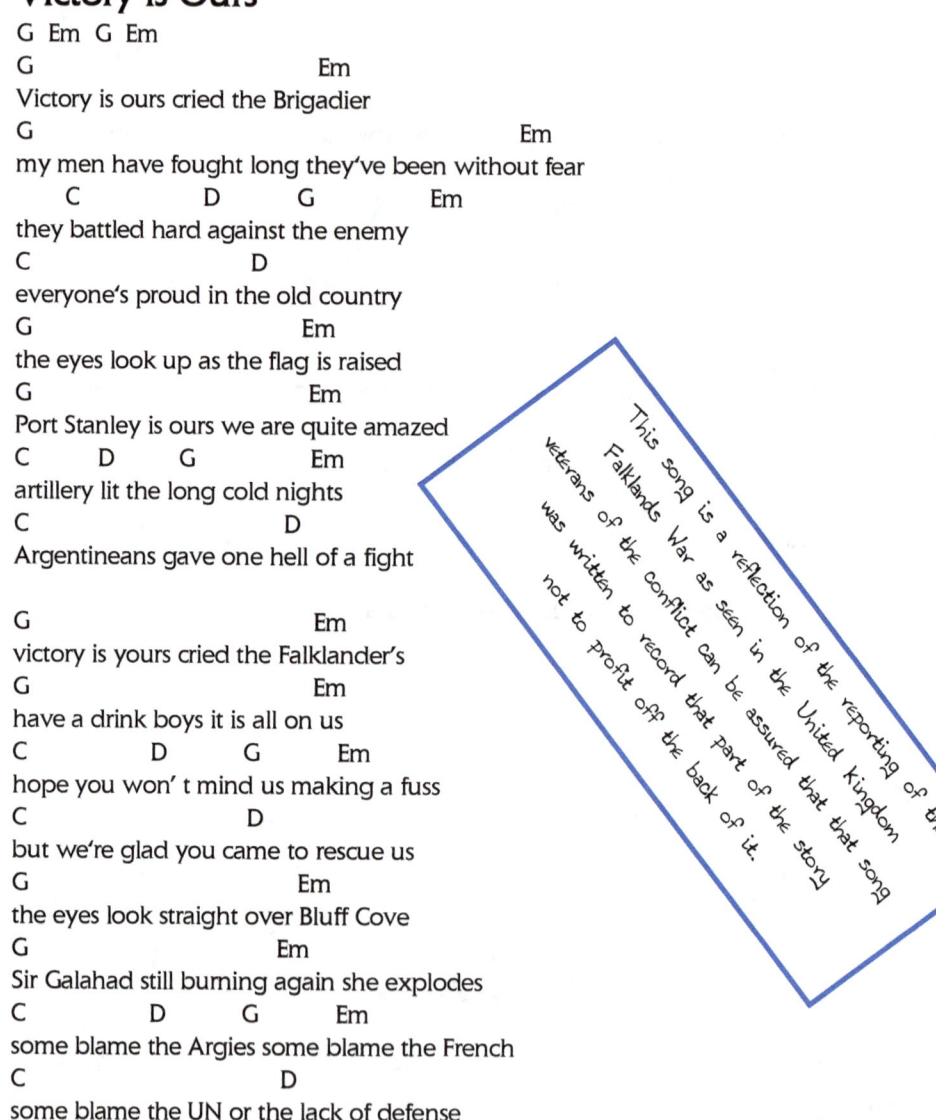

This song is a reflection of the reporting of the Falklands War as seen in the United Kingdomveterans of the conflict can be assured that that song was written to record that part of the story not to profit off the back of it.

I Became What I Wanted To Be

victory is ours the Para cried
he'd like to be drunk he'd like to see his wife
the mountains were cold and he nearly died
his friend was hit how did he survive
the eyes look down in the church now
looking around each head is bowed
thinking of friends who can no longer be here
surely these brave men won't resort to tears

victory is yours the Argentine mother cries
my son was sixteen Galtieri lied
his letter said training in the Andes
he's in a mass grave in the Malians
the eyes look upon his grave
how long must people be slaves
isn't it time they weren't ruled by the gun
isn't it time that their freedom was won


```
      G                          Em
victory is ours the politicians cries
      G                          Em
it was for freedom of course we are right
   C         D       G         Em
if we didn't  protect  your sovereignty
   C                D
       how could you sleep easy
      G                          Em
the eyes have it the vote is passed
      G                          Em
Mrs Thatcher knows her support will last
         C         D   G    Em
           there will be an enquiry
          C                      D
the results will be shown on your TV
```

```
   G                            Em
that's good cried the girl whose fiancé is dead
   G                        Em
they say I am young but am I supposed to forget
     C         D       G       Em
he was strong young and handsome and he loved me
     C               D
if you'd loved that man you'd feel the same as me
     G                     Em
   the eyes loots at the television
        G                 Em
     acts of incredible heroism
  C        D       G       Em
   men who have been trained to kill
     C                  D
   so gentle with their friends so ill


   G                              Em
victories ours the Union Flags are raised

      G                         Em
   we welcome the injured home again
     C         D       G       Em
the crowds throng and the banners are high
        C            D
   as high as the Harriers that flew in the sky
        G                     Em
   the eyes are smiling to welcome home
        G                        Em
   the army the air force the navy marine
     C         D       G       Em
   sorry if you had to stay in the snow
  C                     D
but if you are there a Christmas  it won't be so cold
```

I Became What I Wanted To Be

Just To Survive

  Am
Hiding in those hills is a man with a gun
G   Am
I'm not talking about a riffle more the riffle's great grandson
                                 G
more deadly than a cannon and it's pointing at us all
                          Am
that old red devil has our back against the wall

        Am
*so black man kills white man
G   Am
and everyone dies brother kills brother just to survive

  Am
the Army convoy creeps down the autobahn
            G   Am
but the busy rushing traffic rushes on and on and on
                G
no body sees them and nobody cares
           Am
they are the army and everyone's heard

         *

  Am
hiding in those hills is one of our boys
G   Am
and he's got a button and he's ready to kill
                  G
but everyone knows that they both are there
            Am
they both have the power but nobody dares

MCPS/PRS 323493BS ISWC: T-011.458.310-6 Written 1978

Back In The States

       C   F   C
Back in the States said the GI
G7   C
we've got 52 television stations
  F   C   G7   C
and the stores are open 24 hours a day
F   C   G7   C
whilst out here in Germany you can't get our fast foods
F   C   G7   C
eating a Bratwurst can take you all of the day

   C   F   C   G7   C
*La la la la la la la la la la la la la la la la
   C   F   C   G7   C
La la la la la la la la la la la la la la la la

      C   F   C
back in the States said the GI
 G7   C
we've got everything
F   C   G7   C
we've got the biggest ice cream and the tastiest woman
F   C   G7   C
whilst out here in Germany you can't drink the water
F   C   G7   C
and people don't speak English just like what they oughter

*

I Became What I Wanted To Be

        C   F   C
back in the States said the GI
     G7   C
we use real money
 F   C   G7   C
and lots of the girls are ready to call me honey
F   C   G7   C
whilst out here in Germany the coffee's full of caffeine
F   C   G7   C
and I'm sure the Coke a Cola tastes different here you know

*

        C   F   C
back in the States said the GI
     G7   C
they think I'm patriotic
F   C   G7   C
well the army's better than welfare and they said that I had to go
F   C   G7   C
whilst out here in Germany AFFIES supply the hamburger
F   C   G7   C
my car is new it's tax free and big advantage you know.

MCPS/PRS 323493CR ISWC: T-011.458.310-6 Written 1990

I worked across Europe and out to the Philippines for the American Forces. It was an experience to be in Germany, enter a US Military Base and warp into America. They used American Dollars, ate American food and drove American cars. Many of the people treated me very well. There is not the space here to explain it all. They gave me opportunities unmatched by others I worked for. I am ever grateful.

Thanks Jean Grant

If I Had Done Something Else

    A   G#   G
The Hibiscus whispers to the Cherry tree
    A   G#   G
the Cherry tree whispers to the wind
D#Maj7   DMaj7   C#Maj7
the sun was golden as the evening falls
Em7   A7
the wood fire smoke stings my nostrils as I sing

    G   A   D
and if I had done something else
    G   A   D
if I had gone another way
G   A   D
if I'd been able to turn back the clock
G
there are things that I would change
    A
and others I would not

    A   G#   G
the memory of Michael hangs heavy inside
    A   G#   G
and how I shouted at him
D#Maj7   DMaj7   C#Maj7
his skin was itchy and his body was small
Em7   A7
we were horrid to him did he grow up tall ?

I Became What I Wanted To Be

      A   G#   G
the milk man got up early
A   G#   G
and stole my girl friend from me
D#Maj7   DMaj7   C#Maj7
or if I were to be more honest
Em7   A7
if I'd been different would she have stayed ?

      A   G#   G
I was once painfully married
A   G#   G
but thankfully she went away
D#Maj7   DMaj7   C#Maj7
she left me holding the baby
Em   A7
he's a fine young man today

     A   G#   G
you know that I often tremble
A   G#   G
about words and phrases that were said
D#Maj7   DMaj7   C#Maj7
they send shivers down my spine
Em   A7
and weigh the same as lead

MCPS/PRS 323493CS ISWC: T-011.458.310-6 Written 1992

What Did Mrs Beatie Do

Fm Em Dm Fm Em Dm Fm Em Dm
Wa, wa, wa Wa wa wa Wa wa wa

    Dm   Dm
Oh what did Mrs Beatty do
  Em7   Em7
to have to report to the crew
Bb   Bb
her face was red as she stood up to
  A7   Dm
be spoken to by the captain

wa, wa, wa Wa wa wa Wa wa wa.

Dm   Dm
there were some muffled words and an angry cry
  Em7   Em7
the captain said you're telling lies
Bb   Bb
Mrs Beatty said That's snide
  A7   Dm
show me where's your proof man

wa, wa, wa Wa wa wa Wa wa wa.

   Dm   Dm
there were some angry shouts
   Em7   Em7
and some shoving about
   Bb   Bb
a policeman said grab the lout
A7   Dm
and they huddled off down the gang way

wa, wa, wa Wa wa wa Wa wa wa.

   Dm   Dm
on the land in Muscat in a heat haze
   Em7   Em7
the captain said never in all my days
   Bb   Bb
I apologies and hope that you
   A7   Dm
will fly with us again soon

MCPS/PRS 323493CT ISWC: T-011.458.310-6 Written 1982

Muscat over aeroplane wing

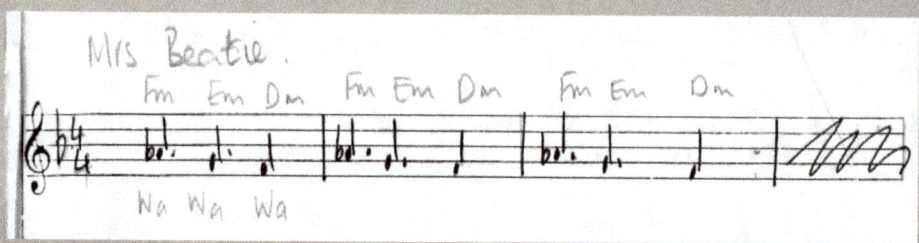
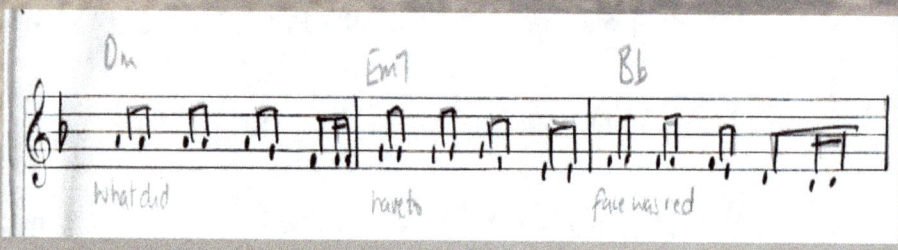
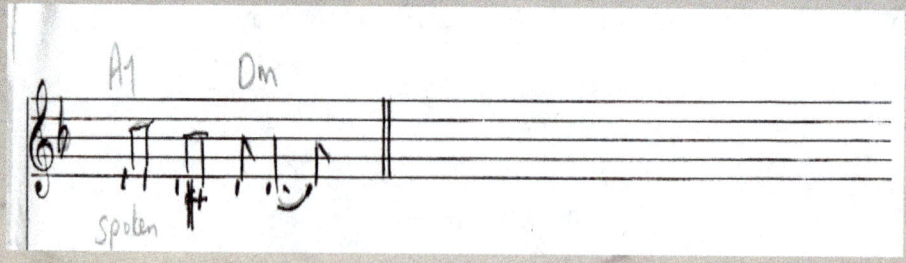

I Became What I Wanted To Be

Raffles Hotel Singapore

Lean On Me Any Time That You Want Too

Use this chord shape of E on the 13th, 12th**, 4th***, 6th**** 1st frets with no bar to produce the guitar part*

F*   E**
She came skiing out of the blizzard
F*   E**
Icicles in her hands
F*   E**
somersaulted above my head
       G***   E
told me I was her new man
F*   E**
I said you're very beautiful
F*   E**
it's that sexy look in your eyes
F*   E**
you can be my woman
       G***   E
with your love I could be satisfied

A   B7   E
*lean on me any time that you want to
A   B7   E
make me laugh every day
A   B7   E
it's my dream to make you happy

I Became What I Wanted To Be

          A   B7   E
in each and every way
F*   E**
she said I have some baggage
F*   E**
from the latter part of my life
F*   E**
I'm afraid of the future
      G***   E
the past was such a fight
F*   E**
I said don't think about it
F*   E**
learn by what is done
F*   E**
we won't get anything
      G***   E
we don't fix our minds upon

                                *

A****
everyone wants what we've got
                            G***
so enjoy holding on
A****
if everyone had what we've got
                            G***
they'd be singing this song

MCPS/PRS 323493CW ISWC: T-011.458.310-6 Written in February 2005

Juke Box Baby

```
C              Am         F              G7
Toss me another peanut and I'll sing another song
F          G7         C     Am
I know all the good ones so you can sing along
   F             G7       C              Am
'cause I'm a juke box baby singing juke box songs for ladies
F          G7         C          Am
they call me juke box singer guitar jokes and all

C       G7      F         G7
fill  another glass and I'll play another tune
F          G7            C      Am
underneath my breath I'm praying my big break will be soon

C          Am    F          G7
pass me another sandwich and I'll tell another joke
F          G7                 C
there were these to Irish men and this other bloke

C            Am    F                        G7
when I'm at the Palladium you will know my juke box days are done
F          G7          C
and I'll be making hits so that you can sing along
F      F      G7       C                Am
to another juke box baby singing juke box songs for ladies
F          G7       C  Am           Am
they call him juke box but I can't remember his name
```

MCPS/PRS 323493CU   Written 18 March 1976

Ray Figg liked my singing and employed me in his pub every Wednesday evening. I did sixty shows for him over a few years. He was kind and gentle and my career may not have been much but for him. Oliver Reed, the actor, used to frequent the pub and he always wanted me to sing 'Mull of Kintyre', the song by Paul MacCartney. Ray bet me one night the first of us to own a Rolls Royce. Then he said "that is cheating as I have already owned one." He said "to me you are like a Juke Box you should write a song called 'Juke Box Baby'"

Anke's Song
(Born 11.3.50 Died 17.11.88)

```
E    B    A         E    B         A
Here I stand looking where you looked
D A      E
beautiful view
D        A
beautiful you


E         B         A    E    B         A
I remember barbeques and restaurants with you
D        A         E
and there were parties too
D        A
beautiful you


E              A
*but did I ever know you
D        A
I can't be sure
E        E
yet I think I did
                    A
as I gaze through your door
D        A
you were so fine
D        A
you were so fine
```

```
E    B      A         E    A    B
```
German was you you spoke French and English too
```
D         A              E
```
you tried to teach me too
```
D          A
```
beautiful you

*

```
E    B       A        E    E A    B
```
Sweden and Norway land of the mid-night sun
```
D         A              E
```
skiing down the mountain
```
D          A
```
beautiful you

*

```
E   B   A       E    A      B
```
did you love ? did that someone love you ?
```
D         A              E
```
I've seen pictures it's true
```
D          A
```
beautiful you

MCPS/PRS 323493BT
ISWC: T-011.458.310-6
Written 1990

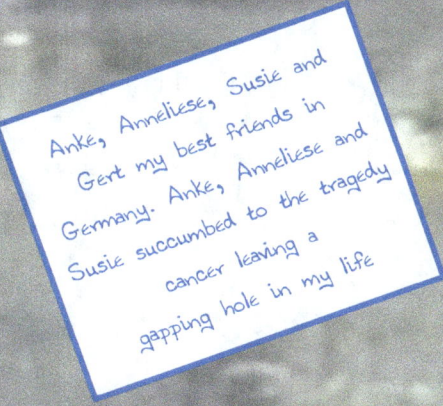

Anke, Anneliese, Susie and Gert my best friends in Germany. Anke, Anneliese and Susie succumbed to the tragedy cancer leaving a gapping hole in my life

Nigel's Song
(Died 20.12.93)

```
  G                         D
I was proud to be your friend
     C              G
and sad when you died
                       D
but I've still got your music
     C              D
and in that you are alive
  G                   D
I will treasure your memory
  C                      G
you meant so much to me
 D       C             D
kept me going through these many years

     C    D    G               G
*Oh Oh Oh you must live your life now
     C              D
you who are left behind
   C          D     G
how many more days left to do
                 C              D
all the things you could do if you tried
```

```
     G                    D
      the Shakespeare's Head
     C                G
        in Carnaby Street
     D                D
      seems so many years
          C       D
        or was it a minute
     G                    D
     it's the treasure of the moments
     C                      G
      as time shrinks and stretches
           D       C       D
     now there's no more time for you

                    *

     G                    D
        Julie Christine you and me
     C                      G
      that horrible Bulls Blood Wine
                            D
        certain of the future
          C       D
        stolen terrible crime
     G                       D
      the treasure of the years now lost
     C                   G
        will remain uncounted
                         D
        but I'll count the beats
     D       C               D
       and sing you one more time.
```

MCPS/PRS 323493BU ISWC: T-011.458.310-6 Written 1993

We Went to Vienna

  C   C
We went to Vienna when we went to Vienna
        G7   C
there was a lady who had henna in her hair

she said that she wore henna to try to catch a fellah
          G7   C
who she didn't think would care

        F   G7   C
*she stood alone by the Prater Wheel
       F   G7   C
such a lot to give such a lot to feel
      F   G7   Am
he walked by she caught his eye
F   G7
he looked like a spy as he lifted his raincoat

C   C
we went to Vienna In the middle of November
         G7   C
I'd never tasted such good coffee

she worked in the café it was near to the opera
        G7   C
she said she only tried to please

I Became What I Wanted To Be

                  C
we were in a horse drawn carriage as they strolled around the corner
       G7   C
the lady with the henna in her hair

I tried to take a photograph of the handsome fellah
G7   C
but someone bumped my arm then there were not there
     Am
     was he a spy was he a private eye
    D7   G
    did his penknife conceal a radio

   Am   Am
was he the real James Bond looking for a blond
D7   G
making do the red-head from the Prater Wheel

Lewis Cedar

*

C
it was the Spanish Riding School the last time I saw them
G7   C
he spoke of security

she asked him if the police would come he said if the game was up
G7   C
it would be the Military

*

C
that was thirty years ago and if you are listening to this song you'll know
G7   C
that the soldiers didn't come

we can only hope that they got married
G7   C
and now they have a daughter and a son

MCPS/PRS 323493BV
ISWC: T-011.458.310-6
Written 1990

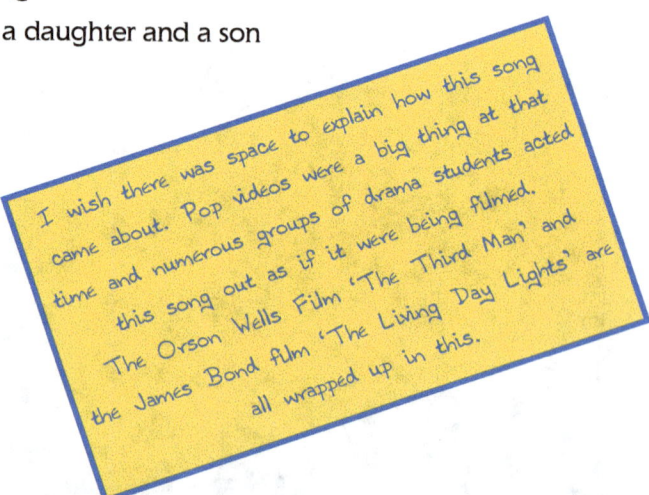

I wish there was space to explain how this song came about. Pop videos were a big thing at that time and numerous groups of drama students acted this song out as if it were being filmed. The Orson Wells Film 'The Third Man' and the James Bond film 'The Living Day Lights' are all wrapped up in this.

Sweet Years

Through the leaves of autumns finery

the sun beams are streaming endlessly

to the river that seams the valley so wide

and as the chill of winters icy hand

touches the shoulder of summers sea and sand

it's October I'm waiting for the first snow to fall

November will soon be here and gone

December brings the Christmas song

another year slips by so easily

through the haze of the summer green

the rain cools the pastures and the dreams

in the mountains still topped with cream

the last spring snowfall

and as the birds that were born in spring

learn to fly the late summer wind

it's September and autumns nearly here again

MCPS/PRS 323493CV ISWC: T-011.458.310-6 Written 01 November 1975

He Gave Her Frangipani

```
C                         C
He gave her the frangipani
D7
she said, "Does this mean I must love you?"
G7                        G7
he smiled at her like a father
C          C
said, "Only if you want to"
F    D7                        D7          G    GMaj7  G7
she looked at him with her solemn brown eyes
C                     G7     G7
she said of course I should love you
F          C
what else could I do
F          C              D7             G7
but I'm undecided though my  father wanted me to
C                     G7
you're strong and you're handsome
F                C
but give me a little more time
F                C
no  don't go away from me
D7                   G7
come here and hold me tight
```

```
C                    C
he looked at the frangipani
D7
he said does this mean you want me to love you
G7                        G7
she smiled at him like a lover
C       C
said only if you want to
D7              D7          G   GMaj7 G7
he looked a her with fire in his eyes
C                    G7     G7
he said of course I should love you
F            C
what else could I do
F       C           D7              G7
but I'm undecided, though your father wanted me to
C              G7
you're brave and you're beautiful
F            C
but give me a little more time.
F            C
no don't go away from me.
D7                G
come here and hold me tight
```

There is a lot I do not understand.
There is a a lot I do not understand about arranged marriage.
I got the idea for this in Brunei and finished it in Singapore.
The Frangipani is often grown in cemeteries there, the girls father
has died and the couple are wondering if they will honour his wishes.

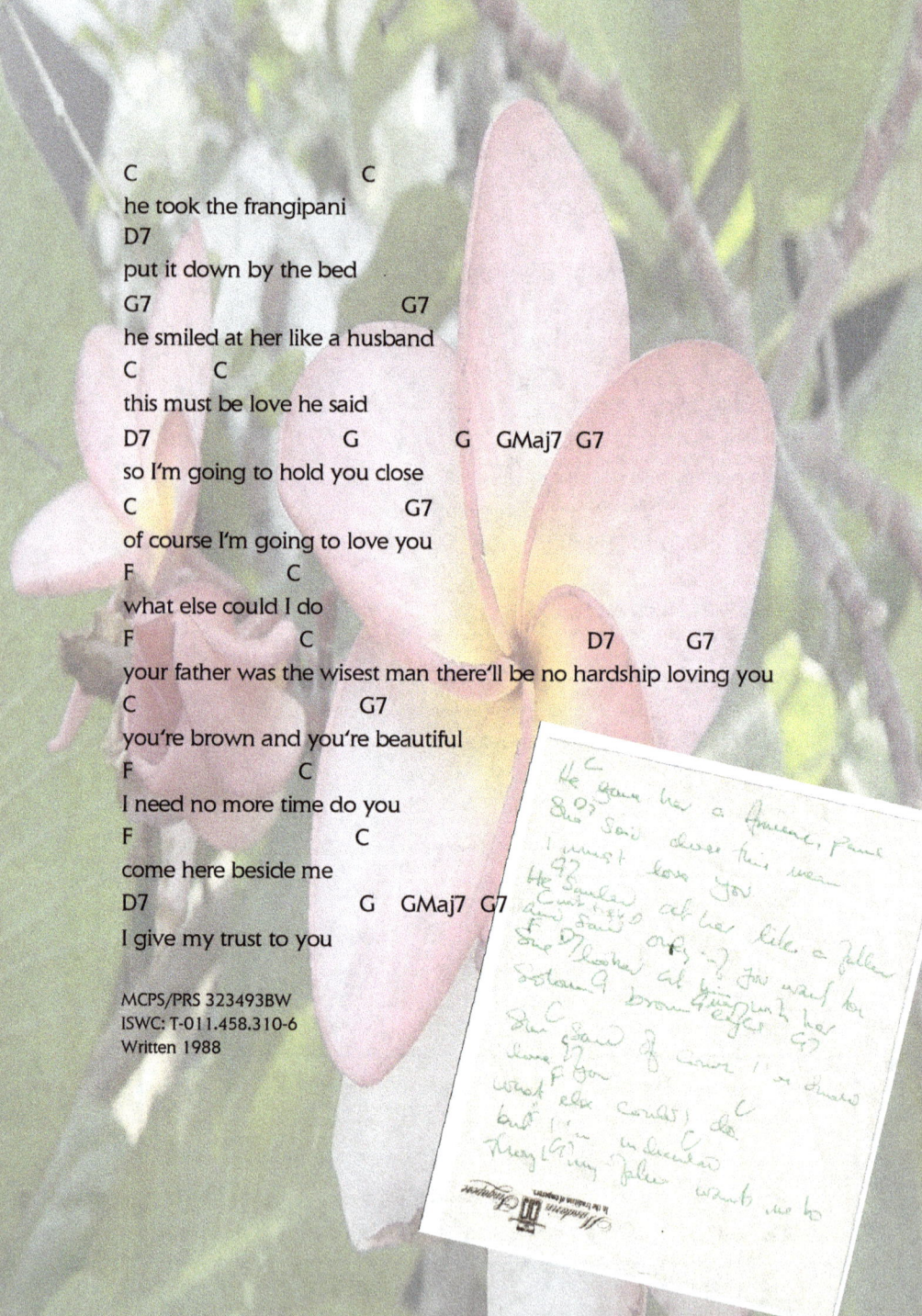

C		C
he took the frangipani
D7
put it down by the bed
G7   G7
he smiled at her like a husband
C   C
this must be love he said
D7   G   G   GMaj7 G7
so I'm going to hold you close
C   G7
of course I'm going to love you
F   C
what else could I do
F   C   D7   G7
your father was the wisest man there'll be no hardship loving you
C   G7
you're brown and you're beautiful
F   C
I need no more time do you
F   C
come here beside me
D7   G   GMaj7 G7
I give my trust to you

MCPS/PRS 323493BW
ISWC: T-011.458.310-6
Written 1988

I Became What I Wanted To Be

Richmond Lullaby

```
  G                    Em
Once I had many friends
  C                      D
they all came to see me
G             Em
I'd planned all my songs
              C
  some were hard
          D           G
and others nice and dreamy
  G                    Em
they all arrived right on time
    C         D
I thought it would all be fine
  G                  Em
they smile and said hello
  C                        D
now come on lets on with the show
  Dm                          G
but the show was over  before it started
```

MCPS/PRS 323493DM ISWC: T-011.458.310-6 Written in 1972

> There have been a few times in my career when I have turned up to do a gig and have found it was cancelled. This was the first time that happened. I took along a gang of friends but the show could not proceed.

Hangs Together

    Dm   F
I am only as polished as my guitar
    Dm   F
I am only as shiny as the wire
C   Bb
this performance is as perfect as the tuning
F   C Am
The sound is as good as the act

    Dm   F
I am only as stylish as her body
    Dm   F
I am only as neat as the strings
C   Bb
this singing is as pleasant as the song is
F   C Am
I am made up of these things

When The Lady Says Goodbye

Single Notes
c d f g   a   ab g
When the Lady says Goodbye
  c   d   f   g
what can you do
  F   C
don't lose all the wonder
              F
You lived through
Bb   C7
it was worth it when you started
  F   Dm
the sacrifice has been paid
Bb   C7
so say farewell I'll miss you
  F   Dm
good luck upon the way

I Became What I Wanted To Be

Single Notes

  c d f g   a ab g c
you did not know it would happen
      d f g
   just like that
  F   C
the whole world
      F
come tumbling down
Bb   C7
it's hard to think of anything
F   Dm
that could turn your thoughts around
Bb   C7
so say farewell I'll miss you
F   Dm
good luck upon the way

MCPS/PRS 323493CN ISWC: T-011.458.310-6 Written 1990

When I was Your Age

```
   Dm              Am7                 Gm
When I was your age the grandfather said
   Bb          F              C
my father had just returned from the war
   Dm        Am7               Gm
and in my day the great grandfather said
    Bb             F         C
   horse and carts passed by my door
            F          C
   and when I was your age my son
         Gm           Dm
       said the father smiling
   Gm              F              A
my heroes were John Glenn and Yuri Gagarin


            F                  C
   do you live your life for tomorrow ?
       Dm                 Am
    do you live you life for today ?
       Bb         F        C
    are you astrologer or palmist
    F C           Dm         Am
  has technology improved the sociology
          Bb        F          C
      or are we head hunters still
```

```
Dm                    Am7                   Gm
who knows what will happen by the time you're twenty
   Bb           F                  C
   will they have built tunnels to the stars ?
  Dm         Am7                   Gm
   will they have computers that can love you ?
         Bb              F              C
will they have cars that can drive their own way home ?
            Gm              Dm
will it rain and sunshine will snow still chill you to the bone ?
      Gm              F              A
      or will we all live in an astrodome ?
```

MCPS/PRS 323493CQ ISWC: T-011.458.310-6 Written 1991

I Could Say That I Miss Annie

   C
I could say that I miss Annie
  F
because Annie's gone away
G7   C
she's gone to Hawaii and that's where she's going to stay
                F
she's gone to Hawaii because she's in love with him
         G7   C
and that's why I miss Annie this spring

  F   C
*I only knew Annie for a while
  G7   C
but I sure miss her smile
 F   C
I only knew Annie for a short time
G7
but when I left I left feeling fine

I Became What I Wanted To Be

    C
now I'd like to go to Hawaii
    F
but what good would that do
G7   C
she didn't say she didn't love me but I knew
               F   F
now she's had her baby and I sure she's happy too
       G7   C
but I wish I could see Annie real soon

          *

    C
now if I ever get to Hawaii
    F
and if I find Annie there
G7   C
I won't tell her that I loved her and I won't say that I cared
                      F
but I'm sill in love with Annie and though some loves may never be
   G7   C
I'm just glad that Annie knew me

MCPS/PRS 323493DN ISWC: T-011.458.310-6 Written in 1981

My Passport Says Planet Earth

```
Em                        Em
I've travelled around the world
Am               Em
and everywhere I've been

I've seen people of every size
Bm               Bm
shape and colour of skin
Em               Em
I've done shows for Royalty
Am         Am                  Em
and other famous in their countries too
Bm                              Bm
but the only thing that I've ever seen is that

Am        Em     Em
they're all the same as you

A                  E
*I'm a citizen of the world
B7         E
How about you ?
A                    E
my passport says planet earth
B7               E
is that your country to

Em               Em
I have been to China
Am               Em
I've flown into India to

and the people who live in Egypt
Bm               Bm
have to eat and drink like you
Em               Em
they don't eat Haggis like the Scots
Am         Am           Em
or snails like French people do
```

                   Bm   Bm
        but you can bet you life if they were hungry
                              Am   Em   Em
        they'd eat a MacDonald's like some people do

                              Em   Em
                       I know a woman in Africa
                              Am   Em
                         she loves her baby son

                        I know of an American
                              Bm   Bm
                       who is proud to be a mum
                              Em   Em
                         I know so many people
                Am   Am   Em
                 who have given their children to war
        Bm   Am   Em
        and still we go on fighting and still I ask what for
                                                          *

                              Em   Em
                       you had to sleep last night
                              Am   Em
                          most people had too

                      and there's more that links you
                              Bm   Bm
                to the other homo-sapiens than divides you
                              Em   Em
                       So why be a Scottish person
                              Am   Em
                       why be English Why be a Jew
                       Bm   Bm
                   there are people all over the world
                              Am   Bm   Em
                  and they're exactly the same as you

MCPS/PRS 323493DP ISWC: T-011.458.310-6 Written in 1993

Lewis Cedar

Mister Producer Make Me A Star

        E
Hey Mr Producer

won't you make me a star

I wanna make big money
       E7
drive a Rolls Royce car
     A
I wouldn't worry
B7   E
but someone told me I could go far

    A E B7

    E
hey Mr Producer

take me as I am

then you can transform me
     E7
into a new man
   A
as long as I get the money
B7   E
I'll do anything in your plan

   E
hey Mr Producer

I want to have a million fans

they'll by all my music
   E7
I'll be the new guitar man
  A
then I will be singing
B7   E
to every man and woman in the land

Written with the help of Nigel Cameron
MCPS/PRS Tune Code 323493DQ ISWC: T-011.458.310-6 Written 1 January 1975

I Became What I Wanted To Be

Norman Newell was a huge part of EMI Records when I was introduced to him. I stood in his palatial apartment in Montagu Mansions London. My feet sank into the carpet and I played a new song I had written about a girl friend and I sitting in a Fish and Chip Shop. His response was 'Beautiful Melody but why on earth a Fish and Chip Shop?' I said 'Well that is what we could afford to do.' Norman I and some of his associates had just come back from a wonderful dinner a steak spread over two dinner plates. (Another night we went out to his Fish Restaurant—the fish were swimming in a tank and you had to choose one and Norman ate Oysters—I had never seen that before.) I wrote this song for Norman. He was so pleased he called me on the telephone and said 'I have written so many songs for so many artists but you are the only person who has written one for me. My pal Nigel Cameron helped me to get the tune, style and rhythm right. Many years later I discovered that Norman wrote the music for lyrics by Philip Green, a song for Tommy Steele's film 'It's All Happening', called 'EGG AND CHIPS' in 1963 the B-Side of 'The Dream Maker'

As Far As Hong Kong

Use this chord shape of E on the 13th*F, 12th*E 4thG, 6thA, 2ndF, 1stNormalE, 8thB, frets with no bar to produce the guitar part

```
                    F    E      F   E    B       F  E
   When you were a little boy I gave  you a peach
       A                    G             F        E
it dribbled down your cheek as we played sand castles on the beach
        F            E           F         E
       and we built a tunnel and a locomotive too
          B                       A               E
       the cop pit and wings of an aeroplane that flew

  A                                          G
  *as far as Hong Kong and as far as Singapore
              A              G
           as far as Dubai and London
  A                                       G
          but now it's time for you to go to school
                  F            E
              and I am on my lonesome
```

*

```
   F     E    F              E         B    E    B
before you went to school I tried to show you
            E         B   E           B
     all the world I hope you understand
  A   A    A                G  F       E        E
some folks are very cold so look out for the nice ones
      F         E         F      E
       it don't matter who you are
    B                    A          E
   as long as you keep trying you can go far
```

*

```
F    E       F           E      B              E
I heard you say to a boy the other day It was your decision
              A    G      F        E
   you'd take the consequences come what may
   F    E    F                       E  F
   I was so proud I wanted to shout it out loud
      B           A               E
   over the roof tops and away into the clouds
```

*

Written in 1992

I Became What I Wanted To Be

Land Of The Filipino's

```
D                        A               D
Far away across the sea is the land of the Filipino
D                        A               D
Polly took a Jeepnee down to see her friend Rodrigo
G                           D
Rodrigo owned the best Jeepnee in town
G                           D
it was every colour and it made every sound
G                        A               GD
had four horses on the bonnet  and a silver plated number plate

D                        A               D
Polly loved Rodrigo like no one had done before
D                        A               D
she looked into his eyes it was she that he adored
G                           D
he wanted to give her everything in the Philippines
G                                     D
he wanted to give her a house that would match her dreams
G                        A               GD
but she lived in a squat hut on the north side of Manila Bay
Em                           D
she was young a pretty expecting his baby any day

D                        A               D
Rodrigo got up early he knew where to steal the gun
D                        A               D
he put it in his pocket and it was down the road he run
G                           D
he looked to the sky and said a Hail Mary
```

I Became What I Wanted To Be

G   D
please understand please help me
G   A   G D
I do it for Polly and for my unborn son
Em   D
but the Bank Guard aimed and fired Rodrigo didn't get the chance to run

D   A   D
now Polly gets up early she goes down to see her son
D   A   D
he's still young but he's grown now and He still loves his mum
G   D
he wants to give her everything in the Philippines
G   D
he wants to give her a house that would match her dreams
G   A   G D
so he's working tomorrow and he'll work again today

D   A   D
far away across the sea is the Land of the Filipino
D   A   D
Polly took a Jeepnee down to she her friend Rodrigo

MCPS/PRS 323493DR ISWC: T-011.458.310-6 Written in 1986

Did You Hear The Spanish Lady

E
Did you hear the Spanish Lady
A   E
she had a tale to tell about Christopher Columbus
B7
 who sailed around the world
E   A
she said that she had known him I asked her how she could

F#m   E
*she said this world is full of many strange things
F#m   E
she took my hand and smiled with the eyes of a thousand lives
      B7
and somehow I understood

E
she said that she'd been a dancer
A   E
and she'd worked on many farms Her husband had been a matador
B7
who unfortunately came to harm
E   A
she said that she'd kissed Franco when I asked her how she could

*

A   E   F#m   C#m
her stories went on forever her sharp black eyes explained
F#m   C#m
that four hundred years ago
    D   D7 E
she was married to the King of Spain

I Became What I Wanted To Be

E
my mouth it dropped right open
A   E
but something said that she was telling the truth
B7
she said that Picasso had painted her whenever he could
E   A
she said that she had loved him when I asked her how she could

*
E
she put her hand in her pocket
A   E
she pulled out a gold Doubloon
B7
she said it came from a Galleon that had sailed about the moon
E   A
it was a mermaids magic and when I asked her how she could

MCPS/PRS 323493DS ISWC: T-011.458.310-6 Written in 1988

She Powers What I Can Be

```
 D              A          G                    F#
My bedroom mystery travelled five homes with me
 D              A          G                    F#
not a ghost  a spirit free  my fortune she stays with me


          G            A            D
         look at a happy man,  look at me
          G    A                D
         she powers what I can be
          Gm         F#         G
         and I am because of her
```

year vanish magically, everyone can see

obvious our children growing splendidly

one plus one synergy the trick to propel you to infinity

the magic deep in her eyes supplies the energy

MCPS/PRS Tune Code 323493DT ISWC: T-011.458.310-6 Written 15 February 2005

I Became What I Wanted To Be

Dream Dream Dream

Use Chord shape D play the top three strings on fret 7 4 and 2
    Dream Dream Dream

Use Chord shape D play the top three strings on frets 5 3 and 2
    Dream Dream Dream

  G   A   D
I dreamt a Mars Bar ate me up in the night
     G   A   D
I gave a tiger a great big fright
    G   A   D
I woke up my teacher was looking at me
  G   A
she said this is not the time to dream but you must

a bigger smile than you wore the day before

you can do better with all of your chores

if you want to live on the moon that's quite possible

all you have to do is dream

I dreamt my Ferrari could fly up in the sky

my girl friend was blonde

she had beautiful eyes

you could eat Mars Bars for your breakfast every day

all you have to do is dream you must

I Hope The Years and You Have Been Good Together

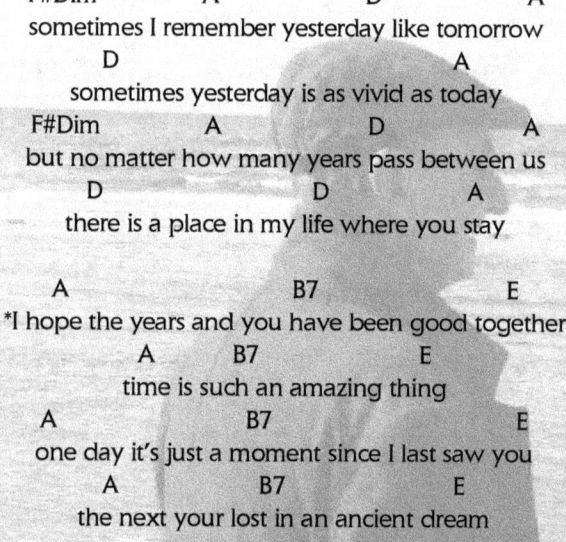

F#Dim   A   D   A
sometimes I remember yesterday like tomorrow
      D   A
sometimes yesterday is as vivid as today
F#Dim   A   D   A
but no matter how many years pass between us
    D   D   A
there is a place in my life where you stay

  A   B7   E
*I hope the years and you have been good together
     A   B7   E
time is such an amazing thing
A   B7   E
one day it's just a moment since I last saw you
A   B7   E
the next your lost in an ancient dream

*

there are people you live with but never get to know

others who share their whole life with you in an hour

you know a handshake that says the owner feels good inside

and the ramblings of the phantasiser

*

Ayr
For John, I owe him my whole career

I have got so much to say thank you for

your singing and playing got me to start

I made up some songs and travelled around the world

with you singing in my heart

*

all these years you've been making people well

I travelled the world with some songs to sell

times were bad and times were good as well

some people were nice and some were hell

*

so all these years have come and gone

took my hair and made you grey

though time is nibbling at our bodies

the friendship has remained

*

I think of you each time I play my guitar

I remember your steady hand and the things you taught me

you're intelligent and kind, the kind of person to trust

with the most secret, secret in the universe

MCPS/PRS Tune Code 323493DU ISWC: T-011.458.310-6 Written 2005

I'm The Boy Who Played Tom Paxton's Guitar

    Am G   Am G   Am G   Am
Richard Lion Heart locked up in a tower
  Em7   B   B   A   E
Austrian's the Holy Roman Emperor abuse of power
  Am   G   Am   G   Am G Am
they passed him to the German's and in Trifels castle it is said
 Em7   B   A   E
Blondel the Troubadour sang and a ransom saved the Kings Head

eight hundred years went by and a new Troubadour

you could say he saved me he inspired me to do much more

I heard his songs as a young boy so I learned to play guitar

It became my life my living and helped me to travel far

    E   A   B7   E
I'm the boy who played Tom Paxton's Guitar
  G#   A
I sang his song, as special guest star
E   G#   A
it took thirty six years of dreaming to do a show with him
B   A   E
'that was a rare treat' he said as I finished it made him grin

That's the Signature Guitar Martin made for you

he said yes how I love it give it a try and you'll love it too

I said you're sharp in control he said I love to do my show

but the travel Midge   my grandsons how they grow

I don't know which of yours is my favourite song

quick as a flash and with that grin he said yes I know I felt the same way for so long

for all these years I sung Tom's songs all around the world

this is to say thanks and look back at a life unfurled

Blondel saved the life of a king, Paxton's words and melodies

saved me from offices and factories

Tom sang of abuse of power of love and many a thing

his music gave me confidence gave me the heart of a king

     E   B7   A
and he shock my hand he made my dream complete

MCPS/PRS Tune Code 323493DV ISWC: T-011.458.310-6 Written 2005

Time To Start Out On Your Own

```
     C            F          G7          C
  You were two  she was gone  how to carry on
        Am        E7            Am
      but we did  and so we lived till now
   C                F    G7                    C
that was twenty years ago  can't remember how many shows
 Am                  E7                   C         Bdim
we travelled around the world   so many stories to be told...and now

             F                       G7
       time for you to start out on your own
                      C
               It's hard for me
                     Am
           but I am proud you've grown
                     Dm
           so strong and independent
                     G7
               so young and free
                     E7
       I wish you every good thing that can be
```

```
     C                  F                G7                    C
   you were eight  time for school   our first big break  powerful
                  Am          G7                Am
                  It changed every role we knew
 C                  F                G7                            C
I found the strength to love again you had to learn my love for you did not end
          Am                   E7                C      Bdim
         hard to grow but in the end  I think you know that its


     C                  F                G7                    C
   you were eighteen  Your friends came by  I sang your song tear in my eye
                  Am          G7       Am
                  happy   you had so many friends
   C                F                G7                         C
   the party went on into the night   I could see you were their  light
  Am                   E7                          C      Bdim
  they were  happy to be with you  and so I could see  that it was
```

Tune Code 323493DW ISWC: T-011.458.310-6 Written 2004

I Was Born and I Was Born Here

```
          A              E          D              D
    I was born I was born here  I'm a threat to no body
                                         A
              and I want no body to fear

              A            B   E   A          B           E
         the night was full of bombs the day was full of fear
    A           B       E              A              E
       my Grandmother and my Uncles  had been dead for half a year
    A                       E       D                        A
    it was dark as he waded through the river my father strapped to his chest
       C7m           B7m              G#°      G#°    A°
          the water was like cutting steel wet the bottom of his vest
         A          E             D                          A
         a single shot rang out then bullets split air from the southwest
         C7              B7                          G#°
         I've been alive for twenty five years and I think that is why
              DMaj7    Db       Em7        A7    Em7  A7
              I never heard my grandfather complaining

              A           B      E    A        B           E
         even when the times were hard and people were so spiteful
    A           B       E              A                      E
    he would turn his head towards them and smile he'd give them an eyeful
    A                    E                 D                    A
       he forged the raging river and walked the mine field the otherside
    C7              B7       B7                 G#°      A°        G#°
    he hitched a ride to near the boarder and  manage to slip passed the guards
         DMaj7  Db'    Em7      Em7                A7              A
         how ? He said I'll never know  I was never so surprised to be alive
```

I Became What I Wanted To Be

111

```
          A    B    E       A         B      A    E
          so a new life among freedom loving people
   A           B     E              A                    E
   no Mosque where he could pray so he happily shared the steeple
         A           E            D        A
         my father grow and went to school  and then into the army
      C7             B7              G#°         A°
      my mother was the prettiest of girls he met at a birthday party
               A         E         D              A
               so I was born into this land I know no other country
   C7             B7        B7                 G#°          G#°
   my skin  a little darker than some of my friends and colleagues
         DMaj7  Db'         Db       Em7     A7A7
         but I speak my mothers tongue and English too
      A     B    E             A       B            E
      many friends since we were five have shared in many intrigues
         A      B     E         A                E
         yet it seems for some people I am the foreigner
      A                E         D                  A
      for those few no matter how I work I am always the outsider
   C7          B7                G#°       A°    G#°   AG#°
   that's their problem but  I wish they had a deeper sense of meaning
DMaj7  Db         Em7                        A7                A
   I think they would walk by an injured man even if he was bleeding
```

MCPS/PRS Tune Code 323493EM ISWC: T-011.458.310-6 Written 2006

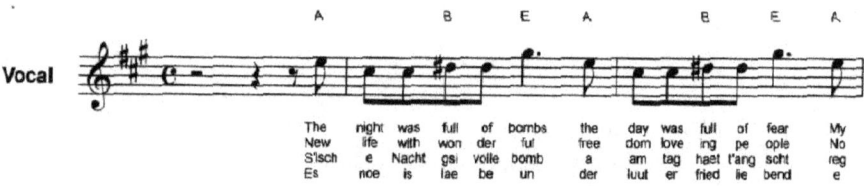
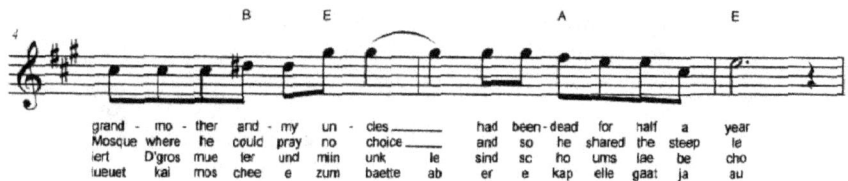

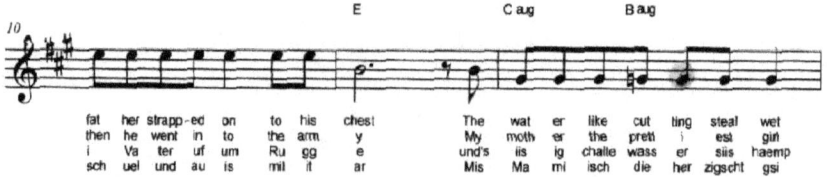

Christine's Smiling Like the Sun in June

    G   D
*Sad times but married again
      C   G
Kenyan Honeymoon
                  D
now Christine's smiling
    C   G
like the sun in June

G   D
when Christine was born her mother said
      C   G
forget jewels and pearls

for I have got the most
D   C   G
precious little girl in all the world

*

G   D
Christine works at the Cash and Carry
G C   G
she sees all kinds of things

a lady said that she had no money
    D   C   G
but wore 5 diamond rings

*

then a man with holes in his pants
fifteen thousand in cash
Christine winked and said to me
I wonder how much more he has stashed

MCPS/PRS Tune Code 323493ENISWC: T-011.458.310-6 Written January 2006

The Gift To Be Free

bbbbbbbbb B7

```
      E                             A                        E
I am so very lucky - to have had your love - all of these years
      E                             B7                        E
I hope you enjoyed the - laughter - you supported - all my tears
    E           A          E          D#         D              B7
like the rocket -  flying to the moon - you were the hydrogen - of my child time years
              A      E     A   E A         B7           E
   and now I'm constantly in orbit I can feel that you're still here

            Dsus4              A                   E
         so thank you for what you have done for me
              Dm7              Asus4
          for taking not much in return
                 D    A     E     A
             I hope that I might be
              Dm7                          E7
        to your grandchildren  what you have been to me
```

```
        E                              A                    E
    In nineteen fifty eight  - you smiling in a - world made of  sun
        E                        B7                E
      sepia photos - old now - you looking so - very young
 E           A         E      E      D#          D             B7
old  super eight  - movies you move and - the camera blinded - by the glare of sun
       E     A     E     A    E    A          B7              E
     and now  I'm constantly in awe of the years, you and everyone


        E                              A                    E
    The very best thing you -  gave to me was the - gift to be free
     E                              B7                           E
   to choose my own thoughts and - my own - truths and to - simply be me
 E           A         E           D#           D              B7
  it takes inner - warmth and confidence  -  to allow another - person to be free
       E     A     E     A    E    A          B7              E
     and now I'm constantly striving to give that which you gave to me
```

MCPS/PRS Tune Code 323493EP ISWC: T-011.458.310-6 Written October 2006

Mrs Beckham

```
         G          C            G
       She said Super Market he said Nightingale
              D             G
              song of fun like Big Blue Whale
           C              G
           wax melting candle flame was done
              D            G
              he was Icarus She the setting sun
           G         C         D7       G
           *he was the Super Market of her choice
        Em                    Am  D7    G
        in far off days shopping for a voice
           F              G
           strawberries and cream jacket of jeans
    D7                F                          C
    up the cut when St Thomas smiled at Beckenham's luck


         G          C            G
         when he hit the Blue Whale his ocean of tears
              D             G
              wet his feet drowning in fear
           C              G
           crash dummy she fell in the ditch
              D              G
              but there was no doctor to make the stitch
           G         C         D7       G
           *he was the Super Market of her choice
        Em                    Am  D7    G
        in far off days shopping for a voice
           F              G
           strawberries and cream jacket of jeans
    D7                F                                    C
    and they drove to see St Joan the Fantail so far from their home
```

I Became What I Wanted To Be

```
G     C                         G
   he fell right through the earth out the other side
                 D       G
            in orbit there to reside
           C              G
         meteor showers cosmic rain
D                   G
light years came and went pure sun don't complain
          G         C         D7      G
         *he was the Super Market of her choice
    Em              Am  D7    G
       in far off days shopping for a voice
         F                G
         strawberries and cream jacket of jeans
     D7          F                       C
   that whisper in her ear was to say that he is still here


   G          C           G
      she was still back on earth caring giving birth
                 D         G
               he a distant memory
            C              G
          but like all good songs come around
            D             G
          until her ear got caught up in the sound
          G         C         D7      G
         *he was the Super Market of her choice
    Em              Am  D7    G
       in far off days shopping for a voice
         F                G
         strawberries and cream jacket of jeans
            D7            F              C
       and every birthday he sat and remembered her
           G        C         G
            so his orbit decade heated re-entry
                D          G
              there she stood a dove of peace
              C            G
                olivewood after this great day
         D                        G
         there was so much more she wanted to say
```

Lewis Cedar

```
        G         C           D7        G
       *he was the Super Market of her choice
   Em                    Am  D7   G
       in far off days shopping for a voice
        F                G
       strawberries and cream jacket of jeans
          D7              F           C
       and every birthday she sat and remembered him

     G      C            G
    frozen can't hold back tears then they were so young
            D           G
           all had changed and then he said
              C         G
             I am the great Super Market
           D              G
          with super life time guarantee packet
        G         C           D7        G
       *he was the Super Market of her choice
   Em                    Am  D7   G
       in far off days shopping for a voice
        F                G
       strawberries and cream jacket of jeans
          D7              F           C
    Scottish Cows and Paddington Bear presents that filled the air

        G         C           D7        G
       *she is the Super Market of his choice
   Em                    Am  D7   G
       in these days they both have a voice
        F                G
       strawberries and cream jacket of jeans
```

MCPS/PRS Tune Code 323493EQ ISWC: T-011.458.310-6 Written November 2006

I Became What I Wanted To Be

Ching Chong China Man

```
  F              C
Ching Chong China Man

  F              C
Ching Chong China Man

     G7              C
Ching Ching Ching Chang Chong

  C        G7
I thought if I dug a whole

              C
        I'd get to China
           F
        I dug and I dug
  C              G7
but China is so far a way
  C              C
   I never got to China
```

So I got on a boat
I thought that I could float
all the way to China
I floated and I floated all day
I came to a country that was far away
but it was not China

Now the years have gone by
and I have grown and yesterday
I was flown all the way to China
it took me a long time to grow
but it was worth it just to go
all the way to China

MCPS/PRS Tune Code 323493EU ISWC: T-011.458.310-6 1976

Oo Char Tra La La

```
F                        C
```
*She said OO CHAR TRA LA LA
```
G7           C      F       C             G7
```
where are you going now I worry if you're late I get in such a state

```
C           G7        F       C
```
Miss Smith had one wish to ease her troubled mind
```
       G7              F            C
```
she showed me her palm said look at my worry lines

*

in the morning she'd read the express the word then Rupert

at getting dressed in her bed she was the worlds expert

*

I put my red Wellingtons under the bed she gave me boiled eggs for tea

she made the greatest chips mashed bananas with top of the milk and sugar for me

*

she filled my head with stories of rolling down the hill

In the afternoons we'd take a walk to see the pigs and the daffodils

          F   C
she said OO goodness gracious me
          G7   C
I find if hard to sleep

   F   C   F   C   G7
I put my ear plugs in my ears but Char's snoring gets to me

 C   G7   F   C
she told me of the war time under the tables they would crouch
         G7   C
but a quarter to two was ding de dong and two o'clock was woman's hour

MCPS/PRS Tune Code 323493ER ISWC: T-011.458.310-6 1984

Game Boy

    F G C

  F   C
In former times
 G7   C
we used to play Cricket
 F C   G7   C
rugby football rackets nets and pitches

  F   G C
that was the Game Boy

  F   G C
that was the Game Boy oo ooy

In times long ago

we played dollies and Maccano

clock-work train sets hula hops and yoyos

In times Ancient

we played cards and hunt the thimble

Monopoly Cluedo Postman's Knock with Wendy Hindle

A *(Bar chord E at Fret 5 then slide it back down to 1)*
but now the little man is running down the road

Pac Man Super Mario Brothers got away

In tImes BC

we used to play the game boy

but now your eyes buzz your ears sting it's the game boy

MCPS/PRS Tune Code 323493FM 1987 ISWC: T-011.458.310-6

Bananas

This is played as a Blue Gras Talking Blues
G C D G

      G
We were eating Banana Custard
      C
back in '58
      D
my Grand Mother Did the strangest thing

as she said doesn't this taste great
G   C
from her mouth and onto her spoon came
      D
a little Banana Stalk

and then to my surprise
                  G
she put it on my plate next to the folk

G   C   D   G
Bananas Bananas Bananas Bananas

G   C   D   G
Bananas Bananas Bananas Bananas

I was about two and a half years old
and I thought Jolly Gee
look what my kind Grandmother
has given to me
I scooped it on to my spoon
and was about to shovel it in
when suddenly she hit my hand
she said you could die of that sort of thing

I can't say that I understood
but boy did my hand sting
I thought she'd given me a present
it was the strangest kind of thing
I tried to explain to my Dad
what my Grand Mother had done
but I don't think he could understand his
crying little son

   C   G
oh she must have been Bananas
     D   G
or mad any way
  C   G
it's the only explanation
D   G
to explain the story away

now all these years have past
since I was two and a half
but I can't say that this story ever made me laugh
and she lived way far across the sea
so we didn't had to talk
but every time I saw her
I remembered that little Banana Stalk

MCPS/PRS Tune Code 323493EW ISWC: T-011.458.310-6 1987

I Can

      E   A
*They said you can't do that
     B7   E
I said I can do that

Open chord of E on 4 3 2 frets
Before I was born

Open chord of E on 4 3 2 frets
They made the rules

    E   A
I was born to early

 B7   E
I thought is was cool

                     *

said I would not live

fevers and chills

double Pneumonia

I got the Polio Ills

                     *

Wilma Rudolf 1960

said I would not walk

let alone run

I decided to Jump

it was a whole lot more fun

*

the Basket Ball Coach

said you're not in the team

you can sit there and watch

you can behave just like the Queen

*

```
        A            B7
          I said Coach
        E             A
  I'm going to be in your team
  B7                          E
I'm going to be part of the Olympian Scene
```

I CAN DO THAT I CAN DO THAT

MCPS/PRS 323493FN   ISWC: T-011.458.310-6   1987

It's Funny How People Can Be

   G   D
It's Funny How People Can Be

   C   D
it's funny how people are

   C   G
you cannot rearrange them
  D
you cannot change them

it can begin with your family

you end up thinking who are they to me

you pull the Christmas Cracker

you leave it under the tree

but then one day when you are in need

you look around you have to exceed

I Became What I Wanted To Be

that what you once had

can no longer be found

you fall in love and you love her

but there is so much more to discover

you find that your defences

have all been blown away

it's all those secret secrets

it's all the truths

that you gave to him

you end up wishing your tongue

had been stolen away

Uncle Percy

```
C                              C
When Uncle Percy came to see me
F                     F
he told me all about his show
G7                                    C
he told me about the day they put him on the radio
                                      F
he told me about his life and times and how many years ago
G7                                F            C
he set his booth upon the promenade and started his first show


F                                C
yes, he made them laugh he made them laugh
   G7              C
he made them laugh and sing
G7                                        G7
because when it comes to Punch and Judy men
F              C
Uncle Percy  was king
```

he told me of his family and how he traveled the world
from France to America Mansion House and Madame Tussauds
and now his sons are Punch and Judy men he told me with pride
he set his hat upon his head he smiled and said "Goodbye"

it was in 1980 that old Uncle Percy died
but Mr Punch and Judy they lived on in a million minds
and for all I know you were one of them who once a little time ago
sat down to enjoy one of Uncle Percy's shows
yes he made them laugh he made them laugh he made them
laugh and sing

MCPS/PRS Tune Code 323493FP ISWC: T-011.458.310-6 1981

Did You Hear About The Man Who Lost His Trousers ?

Open E played at the 13 fret then at 8
Did You Hear About the Man Who Lost his Trousers

Open E played at the 13 fret then at 8
did you hear about the custard pie in his eye

Open E played at the 13 fret then at 8
did you hear about the lady who fell in a puddle

Open E played at the 4 fret then at 2 E
she got mud right up to her eyes

did you hear about the dog who ate bananas

did you hear about the cat who tried to fly

did you hear about t he goat who join the army

her ate all the Colonel's files

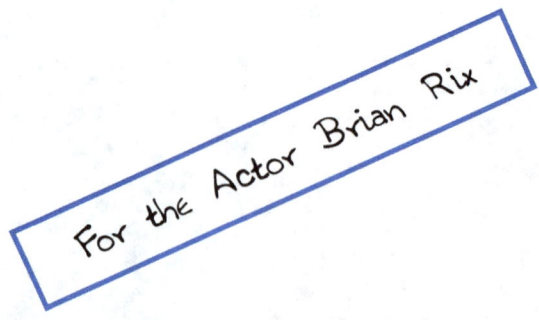

For the Actor Brian Rix

I Became What I Wanted To Be

```
     A                       E
I don't know why your laughing
     A                       B7
  suppose it happened to you
     A                       E
  you say that you can take it
     A                       B7
  but are you telling the truth
```

did you hear about Judith kissing all the boys

did you hear she blow a raspberry in their ears

did you hear about the parrot who lost his sailor

they say that the parrot lost his ears

Time

         B
Click Clock Click went the clock on the wall
         A
click clock click that was it's call
 F#m   E
when along came a digital
 F#m   E
it didn't make a sound
G   A   B
it just crept up there and surprised us all

tick tock tick tock tick

         A
they say it did make a sound
       G
tt would loose a second
B7   E
an atomic pulse was it's heart
B   A
it didn't have hands it was just a row of numbers
     G   B7
and it could speak in the dark   Tick Tock

the grandfather clock goes tick tick tick
the carriage clock goes click click click
but the power went out the digital stopped
and our hero was late for his work   Tick Tock

the Arab man's watch went tick tick tick
the hour glass went drip drip drip
an important client for our hero
but he was late the Arab had to go Tick Tock

MCPS/PRS Tune Code 323493FR ISWC: T-011.458.310-6

Plus Est En Vous-More Is In You

     C   Am
The light from that star

  F   G7   C
Is two thousand years old

  F   G7   C   Am
telescope mirrors focus age and beauty

  F   G7
puzzle reflect think and then discover

   C   Am
what surrounds what is with in us

  F   G7   C
stretch your mind from the extinct

  F   G7   C   Am
understand you are a part of the universe

  F   G7
and this supreme treasure
                          C
there is more inside you than you think

I Became What I Wanted To Be

```
   F         C      Am
plus est en vous plus est en vous
   F            G7              C
there is more inside you than you think
```

fair works sounds and beauty

youth flies upon a breeze

a laser light energising the galaxy

reason harmony and understanding

cherish those who show care for us

let them help us make a link

to people who will wonder around the world

as they look feel and see

there is more inside you than you think

MCPS/PRS Tune Code 323493FS ISWC: T-011.458.310-6

I Became What I Wanted To Be

Lewis Cedar

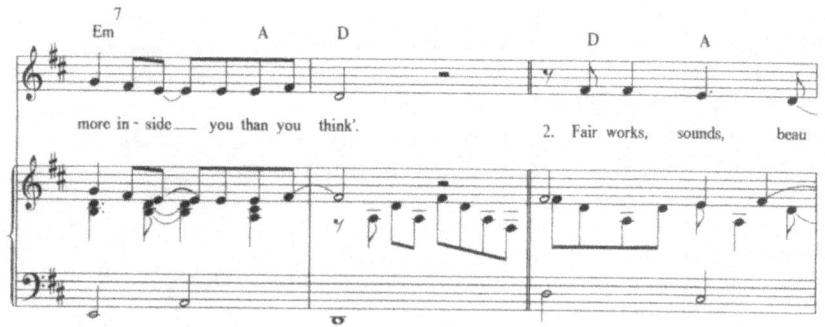

I Became What I Wanted To Be

I Became What I Wanted To Be

Gruuthusemuseum Brugge Belgium

It's Just The Being With You

    A E   D   A
Its just the being with you
 A   E   D   A
doesn't matter what we are going to do
 A   E   D   A
and I hope you feel the same way
      D   E
and that you always will

    A E   D   A
Be beside me everyday
 A   E   D   A
weather your at home or I am away
 A   E   D   A
I want you to always stay
D   E
in my smallest moments and my triumphant day

I Became What I Wanted To Be

     A   E   D   A
and let me be beside you
    A E   D   A
when you win or loose
A   E   D   A
let me be beside you when you choose
      D   E
whatever it is because

    A E   D   A
It's just the being with you

A   E   D   A
what really matters is that when I walk through

   A E   D   A
my memory and my future days
D   E
I see you as you were as you are and will be

    A E   D   A
It's just the being with you
    A E   D   A
all that matters is that I'm with you

MCPS/PRS Tune Code 323654FT   ISWC: T-320.194.317-7 2009

When I'm 63

     C   C
When I'm sixty four you said
  F   F
that was before you married me
G7   C
we'll be sitting here under the Jacaranda Tree
   C   C
I will love you all my days
  F   F
so please marry me
G7   G7
I remember your face

as you waited to hear
G7   C
the replay from me

  F   F
Sixty three years since you walked me
  C   C
walked me down the aisle
F   F
through quilted patches puddles and peaches
G7   G7
oh how you made me smile

I Became What I Wanted To Be

      C   C
ship crossed the equator
     F   F
Neptune silly games
G7   C
with a pillow you knocked that fellow into the water
    C   C
we came to Wales
   C   C
the Jacaranda is Kenya
   F   F
the sunshine is there too
 G7   G7
It doesn't matter at sixty four years
G7   C
I'll still be happy married to you

    F   F
It's just luck if you get the right one
G7   G7
we are still here with our two handsome sons

          20 August 2020

Relax Baby Life's a Choice

   C
When your great great great granddaddy
  F   G7
lived in a cave out there in the hills
  E7   Am
and that old Sabre Tooth Tiger
 D7   G
came sniffing round his door
       C
your great great great grandaddy
  F   G7
either started running
F   C
or he said hey Sabre Tooth
 G7
watch your nose

  A7   D
in life many things happen
A7   B7
understand you have a choice how you respond
 A7   G#7   G7
Pause Smile Question
        C
will help you get along

I Became What I Wanted To Be

when your Dad Dad Dad Dad Daddy
hears the police car on the road
and he checks his speedo
sees the blue light flashing
your Dad Dad Dad Dad Daddy
can start shouting
or he can say in future Officer
I'll watch my nose

when You're self self self self selfish
and your bored in the History Class
and you're dreaming out of the window
and your teacher asks a question
you're self self self self selfish
can stupidly pretend
or you can say sorry Sir
please can you help me with that again

MCPS/PRS Tune Code 323493FT 1996

Rapunzel Let Down Your Hair

    F#m(nobar)   A
Rapunzell Rapunzell let down your hair
D   A#   A
Rapunzell Rapunzell bury me there
          G   F#
in the warmth of your smile
F   E
and the smell of your hair

     A   E
the first time I touched you
           D   A
up in your little room
D   A
and the question you asked
    D   E
I said that I love you

    F#m(nobar)   A
Rapunzell Rapunzell I'm in your charm
D   A#   A
Rapunzell Rapunzell safe from all harm
          G   F#
the light of your knowledge
F   E
for the days of your life

     A   E
and the first time we loved
           D   A
up on that windy hill
D   A
you had me shaking then
    D   E
and I am shaking still

I Became What I Wanted To Be

151

     F#m(nobar)   A
Rapunzell Rapunzell your love and care
D   A#   A
Rapunzell Rapunzell at you I stare
          G   F#
    for so long I was blind
  F   E
  now your beauty is here

    A   E
out from the cold desert
          D   A
I moved with such a speed
  D   A
  I climbed the tower
  D   E
and you are the key

    F#m(nobar)   A
Rapunzell Rapunzell for all my days
D   A#   A
Rapunzell Rapunzell happy always
        G   F#
and now you are with me
F   E
and the witch is away

MCPS/PRS Tune Code 323654FS ISWC: T-320.194.314-4
Written February 2007

Say You Can

    A   E
Say you can and you will
D   A
if your not sure say you'll find out
  F#m   C#m
run for your horizon
  D   E
and always look about
 A   B
*for you only have one life to lead
      E
one hope of winning through
A   B   E
on chance of learning all you can
  A   B
no matter who you are
E   A
no matter where you stand
D   E   Fsus4
your life is there in front of you

I Became What I Wanted To Be

how can you be bored there's so little time

if you don't like it why don't you leave

there's only one person who can live for you

and believe it or not that's you

why do you cry when things are gone

it's just the chance you needed to move on

your girl friends come and your boy friends go

you smile at the old say hello to the new

MCPS/PRS Tune Code 323493FU ISWC: T-011.458.310-6

Councillor Chedwiggen

     Em   Em
Councillor Chedwiggen won't you give me a smile

I'd like your for a daughter but you send me wild

I'd like you to make love to

I'd like you to hug

you feel just like a woman
           A
but you act like a drug

Councillor Chedwiggen won't you raise your eyebrows
I know that I am strong
but I feel just like a coward
I'd like to take you out tonight
and we could paint the town
I'd behave just like a Gentleman
and you could show me round

Councillor Chedwiggen you're figure makes me riled
how can you be on one heap
while I'm on the other pile
I'd like to sit up closer
while the Chairperson clears the room
we could switch the light out
and rid us of this gloom

Written 22 October 1974

I Became What I Wanted To Be   155

I Hope You Will Remember This Song

```
   G            D          C
I hope you will remember this song

     G          D        C
   I won't make it very long

   G            D              C
just to say another year has gone by

G            D           C         D
and still no one else makes me feel so high
```

It's just thirty five years

you and I both know about tears

so we must go on living

so I I can love you

MSCP/PRS 323654GQ ISWC: T-320.194.321-3 19 March 2008

Enjoy The Itch Don't Scratch It

```
      Em                    Bm
   Sir Stanley Matthews they said
      Bm              Em
    when I was a boy


    was the greatest soccer player
        Bm           Em
       a club could employ
 F#    G       A          B              B
 myself I remember Nobby Styles and Booby Moore


       Em                    Bm
    what are the names of  the players

         Bm            Em
        my Son adores

  and as generation slips to generation have we
          Bm              Em      Em
       gained by what they did before
  F#    G          A          B           B
when I am gone will what we did now be thought of or ignored
```

I Became What I Wanted To Be

    Em   Bm
another generation this morning
      Bm   Em
passed away

leaving a whole in time and space
Bm   Em
   that should always stay

F#   G   A   B   B
of a lady a wife with children who led what most would say an ordinary life

    F#   B
she wasn't a Vera Britten

    F#   B
she wasn't a Whilma Rudolf
    F#   B
   she was a teacher
A   B
a person who always praised What she saw as good
  A   B
she sad Enjoy the itch don't scratch it
     B   F#
oh you've done so well

MSCP/PRS Tune Code 675153FR ISWC T-330.459.287-4

Oh You Have A Lovely Voice

G   Am   D7   G
A school boy in the choir
    Em   C   Am   D7
the teacher told the rest to quit
G C   D   G
just listen to this boy sing
C   D
if there were a voice this is absolutely it

G D   G   C
Oh You have a lovely voice
D   G
Oh you have a lovely voice

G   Am   D7   G
he came to the Cathedral
    Em   C   Am   D7
where dead poets lye in state
G C   D   G
and a Queen came and heard him
C   D
she said that the concert was absolutely great
G   Am   D7   G
and then in the studio
Em   C   Am   D7
he was singing out loud clear and true
G C   D   G
backing vocal harmony
C   D
said the producer a voice absolutely new

G   Am   D7   G
and the boy grown to a man
    Em   C   Am   D7
travelling all over the world

Westminster Abbey Choir Stalls

My voice was picked for the school nativity play I was five years old. I liked it. Standing looking at the crowd. Then the deputy head teacher shut the rest of the school up and I sang solo and everyone listened. Geoffrey Smith said come to the Church Choir, I did and so they sent me on to the Westminster Abbey Special Choir and I sat in the pews and the Queen Mother came to hear us. John Spencer and John Pipps came to the youth club and I heard them play guitar and sing the songs of Tom Paxton and I saw my way into the entertainment business. So I spent my life entertaining people. Over twenty countries — I hope that I lifted the spirits of some. Maybe one or two learned something (three Olympic Gold Medallists attended my personal development courses but I do not know if any of what I said to them made a difference). I hope some have enjoyed what I have done.

```
G C     D     G
and always to his surprise
C                 D
people said you have a voice absolutely gold

G    Am    D7    G
years whizzed by internet came
     Em      C    Am      D7
E-mail I down loaded your song
G C     D     G
never heard of you before
C                 D
now I hear your voice so kind absolutely strong


G    Am    D7    G
old Singing boy Came to the hospital
Em                C
his mother's stress shredded life
Am     D7
shocked him through and through
G C     D     G C     C           D
mummy where has your voice gone Who stole it from you


Oh You had a lovely voice


Oh You had a lovely voice

G    Am    D7    G
after twenty seven years His love returned
Em     C     Am       D7
he gazed at her for hours
G C     D     G
he trebled and said
C                 D
through all these years I missed your lovely voice
```

MSCP/PRS 323654GP ISWC: T-320.194.320-2 February 2008

If You Thought That The Rails Were Forever

E   E
When all the inspiration has been dragged from these tracks
    B7   E
the line will be empty and the steel rail cracked

when all the hobos have been here and gone
B7   A   E
all that's left a sleepers and no one journeys home
A   E
*and if you thought that the rails were forever
   A   E
that's in distance but not time
  F#m   F#m
for gone are the old steam Engines
A   E   E
now everything has been streamlined

*

when all the Inspiration disappears behind the bend
the travelling will be over the journey at an end
when all the miles are finished we will be in the border fel
remembering the old steam engines and the tale their whistles tell

*

when all the inspiration disappears from the line
the train wheels will rusty the time table out of time
when all the silver steam clouds fly away to the sky
the fire boxes will be empty the signals block the line

MSCP/PRS 323654GS ISWC: T-320.194.319-9 31 July 1973

31st July

When all the inspiration
has been dragged from these
the line will be empty tracks
and the steel rail cracked
When all the hobos
have been and gone
All that's left are
sleepers
and the one journey home

And if you thought
the rails forever
that's a distance
found not time
for gone are the
Old steam engines
Now everything
Stream line

Hey Holly

This song uses 3 chord sequences
A basic B7 Chord played open at frets 6 4 and 2
A basic A Chord played open at frets 5 and 2
A Basic E Chord played open at frets 4 and 1
A Basic F Chord played open a fret 1 and 3

  B7(6)   B7(4)   B7(2)   E
*Hey Holly what you doing down there
  B7(6)   B7(4)   B7(2)   E
smiling waving your hands in the air
  B7(6)   B7(4)   B7(2)   B7(2)   E
what do you mean you've got nothing to wear
               *

A(5)   E(4)   E(4) E
when your were a baby in the palm of my hand
A(5)   E(4)   E(4) E
I looked at you I could not understand
    F   G
how much I could love you
        *

now you become a young woman
I can't believe that it happened so soon
my hand to
small to hold you
     *

do what you must go where you will
this is your life I hope it gives you a thrill
never let them hold you down

MSCP/PRS 323654FV ISWC: T-320.194.316-6
Written between November 1996 to August 22 2007 Queens Ferry Scotland

Fight the Tide

     A   D
Fight the tide what else can you do

Bm   E
life is a rough ride but you can make it through

F#m   G
use the sunny days to make your self feel good as new

     A   D
get the best from whatever it is you do

G   A   D   G
it may seem funny for a father to say to his son

Em   A
but you're the kind of guy I'd like to become

G   A   D   G
athletic strong clever hansom with a smile to rock the sun

G   Em   A   Em
watching you I think there is nothing you can't become

MSCP/PRS 323654FW 22 ISWC: T-011.702.185-8 August 2007 Queens Ferry Scotland

Marry Me

     G   C
*Won't you marry me my angel girl
     G   D
won't you marry me my love
     G   C
won't you marry me my angel girl
D   G
 you're the only woman I Love
D   G
had enough of living without you
D   G
  had enough of being alone
D   G
it's time that we stopped this fooling
     C   D
  time you moved into my home

*

had enough of being apart of

the lonely hearts club band

it's time that we got together

and started our own Band

MSCP/PRS 323654GM ISWC: T-011.688.023-9
August 1976 Boscombe Beech Christchurch Dorset

My Your Life Be An Apple Crumble

```
       E                        B7
May your life be an apple crumble
                            E
    may you always surf the wave
                         A
may the goddess of the surf protect you
     E B7                    E
 in the gold coast of your new home

 A       E      B7                   E
wherever you go there's always something of you here
          A                    E
    you've been so gracious and kind
           B7         E
         over these years
```

if snow falls on the Albis

we'll think of you in the sunshine

surely these thoughts will melt all the snow

and leave us feeling safe and warm

may your life be a paradise bounty

may it be a plate of blue cheese

may the freshest salad always surround you

in Sydney Melbourn or Brisbane

Three Pretty Ladies

    a   a   a   g# g#   a   a   a   e
Three Pretty Ladies came to my show

a   a   a   a   g# g#   g# g# a   a   a   e
   Where they went to afterwards I wonder if you know
  A#   A   A#   A
I hope if was to a Paradise where the sea is turquoise blue
A#   A   A#   A
  and the sand is so fine it tickles your toes in your shoe

Em   A7   Dm7   C
down among the rocks along the shore a baby feels the pain
  Am   D   G   A7
to little food to little rain In a world that is so full
       D   G
where there is so much to gain
  Em   A7   D   C
there are still many folks who need a daily cup of grain

  A   G   A   E
I hope that they found much love there fun and people who
 A   G   A   E
live in peace because many are unable too
A#   A   A#   A
hope they have good things to eat and enough to fill them up too
  A#   A
pretty things pearls to wear
 A#   A
and flowers all around them too

I Became What I Wanted To Be

```
      A                    G         A              E
    these Pretty Ladies live in the richest land around
      A         G                A              E
    where life hardly rocks if the share prices are up or down
    A#            A              A#              A
    where cars and clothes and gadgets smoother every scene
         A#              A             A#
           the world is full of fat and thin
                         A
                  rich and poor and mean

      A         G                   A              E
    Often wondered why the world for some is absolutely cruel
           A         G             A           E
           Often wondered what more I could do
    A#            A              A#              A
    Why are their murderers and rapists and other prisoners to
               A#            A
            movies escape through fantasy
               A#         A
              Join religion too
```

MSCP/PRS 323654GT ISWC: T-320.194.323-5 Written March 2008 June 2009

Super Sea Morning

```
   G                  G
It's a super sea morning
   D                  D
the sunlight in your eyes
    D                              G
and I woke up today with a beautiful surprise

    the weather forecast was wrong again
         D              D
    but that was our delight

    the day will be happy
        G                G
    I'll see you again tonight
      C                               C
    and I'm proud to know that you'll be there
       G                    G
    I'm proud to hold your hand
       D                     D
    and some time in the future
        D                 G
    we'll lay down in the sand
```

it's a super sea morning
the sunlight in your eyes
and I woke up today with a beautiful surprise
the hours will seep into us
as we sit there in the bright
holding close together waiting for another night

31 January 1974

St Tropez

The Forth Bridge Song

             A Asus4 A
A   A
I carry the Road to the North standing tall in the Firth of Forth
     D   G
I'm strong against the wind and I'm high above the sails
    Bb   G
of the yachts that pass beneath this Bridge
     D   G   D   G
*Oh Oh where do you go oh oh where do you go
     D   G   D   G
Oh Oh where do you go oh oh where do you go

I bring them back from the South standing tall in the Highland mouth
I'm high against the stars and I'm small beneath the Grampians
that roll North of this Bridge

I link the Highland to the low my roadway way arched like a bow
I'm strong against the weather and I stand in the heather
that grows around this Bridge

Macbeth, Wallace, Prince Charlie, Calendionians Pics Crathunie
from Sterling to the Estuary Linthgow through the centuries
the rocks beneath this Bridge

The tropics of Inverasdale, Peterhead the Doric Herring for sale
Aberdeen and the oil Caithness to the border
the people the life of this Bridge

The Carolinas North America Nova Scotia Ontario

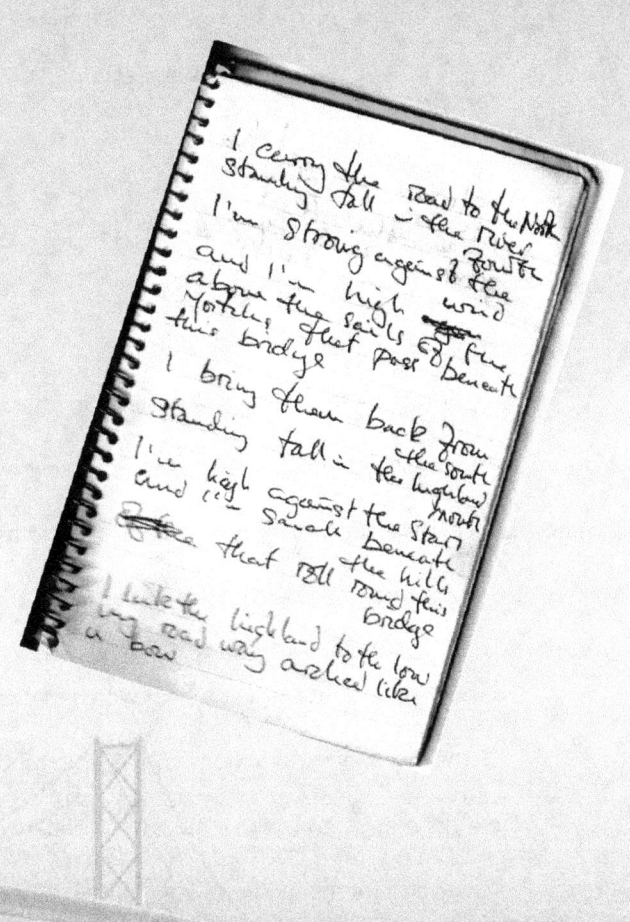

Two thousand and fourteen the ending or the middle of a dream
straight −jacket devolution Independence the solution
green power water we must go

MSCP/PRS 323654GR ISWC: T-011.458.307-1 4 August 1974 Queens Ferry and Falkirk Scotland

Thee Firth of Forth Scotland

Sing It One More Time Again

eeffedddeedc

```
        C   F   G7      Bb      A       F
     I was nearly eighteen when I fell in love with you
        Dm          G7          C           G7
     I was already writing songs but now they were for you
 F              G7              Em              A7
and I sang in the hope you'd love me and I sang to try and make you stay
        Dm7         G7          C       Dm      G7
     you are my inspiration faster flowing than the river Spey

        C   F   G7      Bb      A       F
     is there an ancient language with words that can express 13
        Dm          G7          C           G7
     the inside of my emotions and all your tenderness 14
 F              G7              Em              A7
     I'm a slovenly scholar with a meagre dictionary in my brain 18
        Dm7         G7                  C       Dm  G7
     searching for the medieval imaginary land Cockaigne 16

        C   F   G7      Bb      A       F
     so we sail on a sea of Green through a silver night
        Dm          G7          C           G7
     I'll be making songs about you for the rest of my life
 F              G7              Em              A7
I am away past my half century now and staring right back down the track
        Dm7         G7                  C       Dm  G7
     it feels like you are still seventeen and wish we could go back
```

I Became What I Wanted To Be

      F   G7
and sing it one more time again
      F   G7
with a super new middle eight
      F   G7
but then I miss a beat pause
      F   G7
and wonder if the song would be so great

F   Am F   G7
I hope when I'm gone someone will sing these songs of mine
F   Am F   G7
I hope they will know you inspired all my best tunes and rhymes
    F   Em   Dm7   Am   C°   G
if I could make it clear to them that Greater than the Dynasty Manchu
    F   Em   Dm7   Am   C°   G GMaj7 G7
the best part of the history of my life was my love for you

Emperor Shunzhi 'Son of Heaven'   30 October 1644 Manchu Dynasty or 'Qing' meaning Clear
Feb 12 1912   1645 –1912 Chinese Manchu and Mongolian
Written 9 Feb—9 March 2009

Knight At Your Round Table

B A G F#

```
     B                                    F#
You were the Damsel at the top of the tower
     E                                G#m
I was the wounded knight come to save the hour
         D#m                  C#m  B         F#
the pain had been there for so long my spirit was raw
     E                           G#m
I thought that you would cure my deep wounds
         A                             B
but your long nails went in hard and they tore
```

I was the King sitting at your great round table
built you this castle put horses in the stable
we had parties and feasting in the Banqueting Hall
damsel turned Queen were you listening
did you decide you would not hear my call

```
       B          F#              B
there was a time I wanted to kiss you
    B            F#               B
there was a time when I would really miss you
      E                   G#m
those times now light years away
      E                        G#m
black holes in the star dust beyond the Milky Way
```

I did my duty producing heirs for to throne
you usurped me new powers new laws changed our home
you imposed iron rules and a chastity belt
it frustrated me and innocent
you smashed the table and all I felt

how many times how many words did I get wrong
a decade in the mountains I got snowed on
and it rained an avalanche of your complaints
I was the wounded Knight from your round table
rescued you Damsel from the tower As in an ancient Fable

```
        E                         B
you asked is Who is  Benizire Bhutto
          E             E
           is  the sun a star
        E                  B
     is Mars nearer to the sun than Pluto
```

Written February–June 2009

By Evrard d'Espinques - Gallica, Public Domain, https://commons.wikimedia.org/w/index.php?curid=24915213

The Highway Man

```
Am                  Em              Am
The  night cloured black to the break of day
                        D7     Em
    The day followed after the dawn
    Em          Am              D7  G
and the picture I'm sending you is quiet true
        Am          Em          Am
    for a man with the road in his eyes
        Am          Em          Am
    for a man with the road in his eyes
```

    the day followed on till the evening
    the dusk gave way to the Dawn
and the picture I'm sending you is quiet true
    for a man with the road in his eyes
    for a man with the road in his eyes

    the night hurried on it's stormy flight
    i seemed the dust came of of the moon
and the picture I'm sending you is quiet true
    for a man with the road in his eyes
    for a man with the road in his eyes

```
    Em              Am              Am
    so I rode on past the streams and the valleys
            Em              Am
        I rode on through the glassy night
    Am              Em          Em
    my grey white steed all covered in bruises
    Bm          Em    Bm          Em
    they will not catch me  till the break of day
    Bm              Em  Bm              C
    they will not catch me till the break of day
```

                Written 1972/1973

I Became What I Wanted To Be

Capo on 5th fret — Dm = Shape Am

I Say You're Beautiful

```
   A                    E
I say you're beautiful you say I'm out of touch
         F#m        E
    but yours is the face I love so much
      A                 E
   I can't think of another  that thrills me so
   F#m                 E           E
your beauty is inside out  and out side in it glows

       A                 E
     I love you and the body you dwell in
         F#m         E
     both are wonderful and exciting
       A              E
     I love to watch the things you do
   F#m              E
and hear the words of the day you've been through


          D       E    E    A         F#m
      *when I think of you it's like sunshine shining on the sea
  D                  E                        A          F#m
for all these years you're more than all the drops of  water in the sea
```

I Became What I Wanted To Be

```
   A                              E
I say your good and kind  you say I don't think so
                  F#m       E
you're muddling me with someone else that you know
       A                  E
   and I look in your eyes see the smile so deep
      F#m            E
      I plunge right in  swim in your modesty
```

MSCP/PRS 323654FU ISWC: T-320.194.315-5

The Traveller

```
F                    C
   Me I'm going to Bavaria
F                    C
       every single night
F                          C
I'm going to a castle somewhere
         D              D
          you can play piano
                     G7
            though out the night


         C              Am
       All the way to Australia
         C              Am
discover what you have at home
         C              Am
someone said you'd be content now
         F              C
         I said look at my phone
         C              Am
    WhatsApp message from Corsica
         C              Am
     another from Paris in France
         F              C
 not so long ago it was Vienna
         D7             G7
       oh how you could dance
```

```
C              Am
What was it Tasmania
C                      Am
that's a large jewel in your crown
C                      Am
in Belize was surf and white sand
F                C
Pippi Langstrum knotted sheets
C           Am
open window and gone
C           Am
riding horse through snowy night
F           C
now life's mot easy
D7         G7
how was Veitnam

C              Am
the Empress Elisabeth
C                Am
she was not such a happy soul
C           Am
but she reigned over Austria
F                C
it was forty four years
C                  Am
her childhood was unstructured
C           Am
and totally unconstrained
F                C
she travelled all over
D7         G7
so you got your name
```

July 2020

Man With One Shoe

```
     C              C
  I have no idea
     C              F
   said the man
    G7             G7
   I've been told
    G7       Am
   it's everywhere
    F               G7
 let me look at that plan
    C              Am
 maybe I will understand
    F              G7
  for I gave all I could
     C        Am
 I gave more than I was asked
    F              G7
   three times in my life
 Am                   Fmaj7
 but I could not make it last


   F  G7  C         C
 love love what is it to you
   F  G7  C         C
 love love I gave it to you
   F  G7  C        Am
 love love it broke me in two
   F              G7         C
left me walking like a man with one shoe
```

```
       C              C
Sometimes you see
       C         F
    a lost shoe
  G7            G7
 on the highway
  G7            Am
you wonder from where
    F            G7
 it belonged to a man
 C               Am
who escaped from the crash
    F            G7
cause when his woman left
        C         Am
   him for another man
       F         G7
   for sex and money
Am                   Fmaj7
you ask about the children


   F  G7  C        C
love love what is it to you
   F  G7  C        C
love love I gave it to you
   F  G7  C       Am
love love it broke me in two
    F           G7         C
left me walking like a man with one shoe
```

Lewis Cedar

      C   C
well I am confused
      C   F
Mum and Dad
G7   G7
were not like that
G7   Am
for life they were true
F   G7
only a paper map
C   Am
we had sat navigation
F   G7
they travelled the mountain
C   Am
we sped down the highway
F   G7
their horse found the path
Am   Fmaj7
our Porsche crashed the mountain

  F G7 C   C
love love what is it to you
  F G7 C   C
love love I gave it to you
  F G7 C   Am
love love it broke me in two
F   G7   C
left me walking like a man with one shoe

PRS for Music Tune Code 323653AQ 2016

I Became What I Wanted To Be

Routes De Soleil

            C
We're on our way down the Route De Solie
 G7   C
   to have us a little sunshine

there were Germans a Belgium's Dutch people too
 G7   C
  the Italian's bought their own wine
 E7   Am
*so it's bon jour good morning
 E7   Am
  guten tag good day a a ay
  E7 Am   D7
oh papavore the Spanish shout
    G
Hoo—Lay

we're storming through Nougat and Toulous
that reminds me we've got to go
there were motor cycles caravans mothers pushing prams
and a roller skating baboon

*so it's bon jour good morning
guten tag good day a a ay
oh papavore the Spanish shout
Hoo—Lay

we're on our way down the Route De Solie
to have us a little holiday
there Swedish People Norwegian
Danish people who bought their own cheese and it was blue ... pooh

PRS for Music Tune Code 323654DT ISWC: T-320.194.296-9

King Fisher

   G   G
I never seen a King Fisher Mama
   A   A
I never been to the moon
D   D
I never sailed the Mississippi river
  C   G
I never played a bagpipe tune

you'll the there in your flowery hat Mama
    A   A
on Saturday afternoon
D   D
standing there with your big sister
    C   G
my Aunty June

  C   C
and I'll be married
  G   G
you'll be happy
A   G
I know you'll be sad
C   G
but you know Mama
  F   G
it won't be so bad

```
       G                        G
I know it's not been easy Mama
         A              A
     you had to work so hard
 D                            D
you never climbed to the Coliseum
         C              G
   you never made a deep sea dive


you've been my only parent Mama
         A              A
       since I've been alive
 D                            D
    and look you did a good job
             C       C
        after all I'm still alive


         G                     G
 you never been drag racing Mama
         A              A
   you were never a mother in law
 D                            D
    you never rode on an elephant
             C          G
           never been to Kenya


     I'll never say good bye Mama
         A              A
        you'll never be alone
 D                            D
someday we'll sail the Mississippi river
             C       G
     may be we'll see a King Fisher
```

July 2020

Pyjama Game

```
      E                    B7                        E
Alan and Anne were retired  they loved their routine
                    A           B7             E
a cup of tea and a movie could make a day serine
     E                     B7                       E
in earlier times Anne was a teacher and Alan the local doctor
              A           B7                       E
every Sunday morning  they were first at the Baptist Church door
```

```
 F#m                  G#m  F#m                    G#m
the great thing about a DVD is you can watch it with your friends
  C#m                   G#m  F#m                  E
but the best thing about a DVD is you can watch all over again
```

every Saturday morning Alan went to the Super Store
after buying the groceries he'd look for a DVD bargain from the basket by the door
this week he found a beauty to reminded him of when he was a boy
the Pyjama Game was a classic the thought of Doris Day made him quiver with joy

Anne was busy in the kitchen making a nice cup of tea
Alan ripped through the cellophane his heart pounding with glee
his sweating hands were shaking as he pushed the buttons on the remote control
he missed the title sequence Anne said I have a nice buttered roll

the screen was filled with colour, funny thought Alan it was black and white
Anne said Alan where are their Pyjamas ? That young man just gave me a fright
Alan said Anne, they are naked, I was a doctor I know of these things
but don't I remember Doris and Sid Sorokin doing such exciting things

Anne said oh Alan I fear this is not the Pyjama Game
it seems to be in Italian and look they are doing it again
Alan said I don't believe but we must watch it to the end
on Monday I'll return it to Safeway but on Sunday we'll show to all our friends

I Became What I Wanted To Be

Bad Boy

  Em   Am
Bad boy you naughty boy you're the bad-est boy I've ever seen
  Em   Am   Em
and your so horrible I can't believe you're forever making a scene
      F   C   F   C
Oh but I like Stephen he's been a good friend to me
    F   C   F   G7
he plays neat football and tells lots of jokes to me
Em   Am
come here boy you flicked ink on her dress you're going to loose your recess
Em   Am
and if you answer me back again look at your book it's such a mess
     F   C   F   C
oh but Stephen loves his Grand-Ma-Ma
    F   C   F   G7
helps her do the dishes and polishes her car

    Em   Am
as far as I can see the boys a mess he's rude disobedient
                    Em
and the physiatrist says that he is a mess
  Am   D7
where going to get his Father and Mother up here and what will they do
    G   C
For you tried every trick it says in the book
   G   D
the only thing you didn't do was to write a new book
     F   C   F   C
did you see Stephen helping the little kids
F   C   D7   G
he had such a smile on his face He showed them how to build the bridge

PRS for Music Tune Code 323654CP ISWC: T-011.458.261-4 Written 1989

Chain of Freedom

```
     E        B7          A              E
Caledonia Caledonia sing along with me
                       E              B7
              Caledonia Caledonia
                       A              E
              Chain of Freedom set us free
                       A              E
              Siobhan spoke to Judith
                  E     B7             E
              She said back in the old country
   F#m            G#m         A           B
they made a chain of humans  despite the tyranny
   A                E      B7            E
two million stood hand in hand across three countries
   G#m       F#m     E                 B7
     to show the world  they wanted to be free


                            A              E
                     Wilma said to Judith
                         B7             E
                     I like the way that sounds
                         F#m           G#m
                     we'll make a chain of Scots
                            A         B
                     they'll come from every town
                            A              E
                     seventy-five thousand Caledonians
                            B7             E
                        standing hand in hand
                            G#m      F#m
                     to demonstrate to the world
                            E              B7
                        Independent Scotland
```

16 July 2023

On 14 October 2023 over twenty thousand Scottish Independence supporters held hands along the Forth and Clyde Cannel from Bowling in the south to the Falkirk Wheel in the north. It was a huge demonstration of the the desire of many Scots to live in their own Independent country once again. So many Scots fail to understand that to remain continually doing the same things means that outcomes cannot change.

Chocolate Milk

  C
    Oh I like chocolate milk on a Saturday
    F
    I like chocolate milk on my holidays
        G7
    creamy dairy milk
      C
    chocolate to the hilt
  F   G7
I could drink it until it came out of my ears

I've had chocolate milk in the Philippines
they say there's chocolate milk in Los Angeles
I've had it in Norwich where I didn't like the spinach
but chocolate milk chocolate milk is fine by me

the next time you come round to my house
don't expect me to give you a cup of tea
because I'll reach for the fridge
and I'll life up the lid
and pour you a nice glass of creamy chocolate milk

PRS for Music 323654FQ ISWC: T-011.367.791-0 Written 1985

I Became What I Wanted To Be

Elephant Parrot and Kangaroo

```
B                       A
Last week walking down our street
G                              F#
I saw an elephant he had purple feet
B                   A
looking at him I asked him how
G                              F#
he said look here son  don't be nosey now
B                       A
said I've been walking for many days
G                                  F#
I can't find the jungles from whence I came


B
so I said come home with me
E
we can have tea
F#                      B
we can have cake and strawberries
B
so I said come home with me
E
we can have tea
F#                      B
we can have cake and strawberries
```

I Became What I Wanted To Be

then the other day going to school
there was a kangaroo
breaking all the rules
the teacher told him to go away
he turned to the teacher as if to say
I've been going for such a long time
It's Australia that I've been trying to find

then the other day I got on the bus
and to my surprise sitting next to us
there was a parrot
he had golden wings the conductor
said where you going
the Parrot said I'm looking for Old John
but he's a Pirate and I think he's long gone

PRS for Music Tune Code 323654CT ISWC: T-011.367.892-4

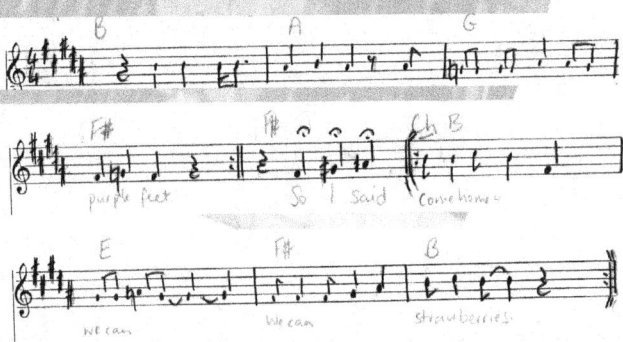

Granddad's Car Horn

G   C   G
When the wheels fell off of my granddad's car
                   C   D
my granny said that's why he never went far
        G   C   G
but he was the only young man she knew
      C   D
who's car horn could go
       G
Toot Toot Toot

C   G   C   G
*Oh my granddads car horn blow all day
   C   G D   G
you could hear it miles away

my daddy owned a racing car
it was shiny red and had chrome bumper bars
do you know where the horn came from
yes it was my granddad's One

now I own a Bicycle it has yellow handle bars
it's a racing one as well
you know it doesn't need a bell
my granddad's car horn makes it go really swell

Go to Singapore

```
      E                         B7
When I was in China there was a China Man
      A                        Gdim
   who said I should go to Japan
         E              B7
    and there I met the only man
         A           E
       who was very poor

                          B7
    *and he said go to Singapore
         A           E
        go to Singapore
                           B7
   and when I asked him what for
              A              E
     he said You have never been
```

when I was in India near the Taj mal hal
I saw a sign leading to Bengal
and there I met a tiger
and I pulled a thorn from his claw

when I was in London
there was a Policeman
who said that he had reason
to believe that the Mahican
had a head that was very small

PRS for Music London Tune Code 323654CU ISWC: T-011.367.784-1

Singapore

He Just Wanted To Fly

```
   C         Em         Am          G7         C
I knew a boy who said he could fly, fly up in the air
   C         Em         Am          G7         C
the silly fool broke his ankle jumping of a chair
            F          G7          C
         *But I never heard him cry
            F          G7    C
         he just wanted to fly
         G7                              G7
      I'm sure he should have been a bird
            F                           G7
      but he's a sailor now it's quiet absurd
```

when his ankle got better he sat on a swing and swung up to the sky
he jumped off the swing it hit him on the nose and gave him a black eye

when his nose got better he stood on the table and he flapped his arms
he ripped his shirt as the table toppled over and broke one of his arms

PRS for Music Tune Code 323654DM ISWC: T-320.194.291-4

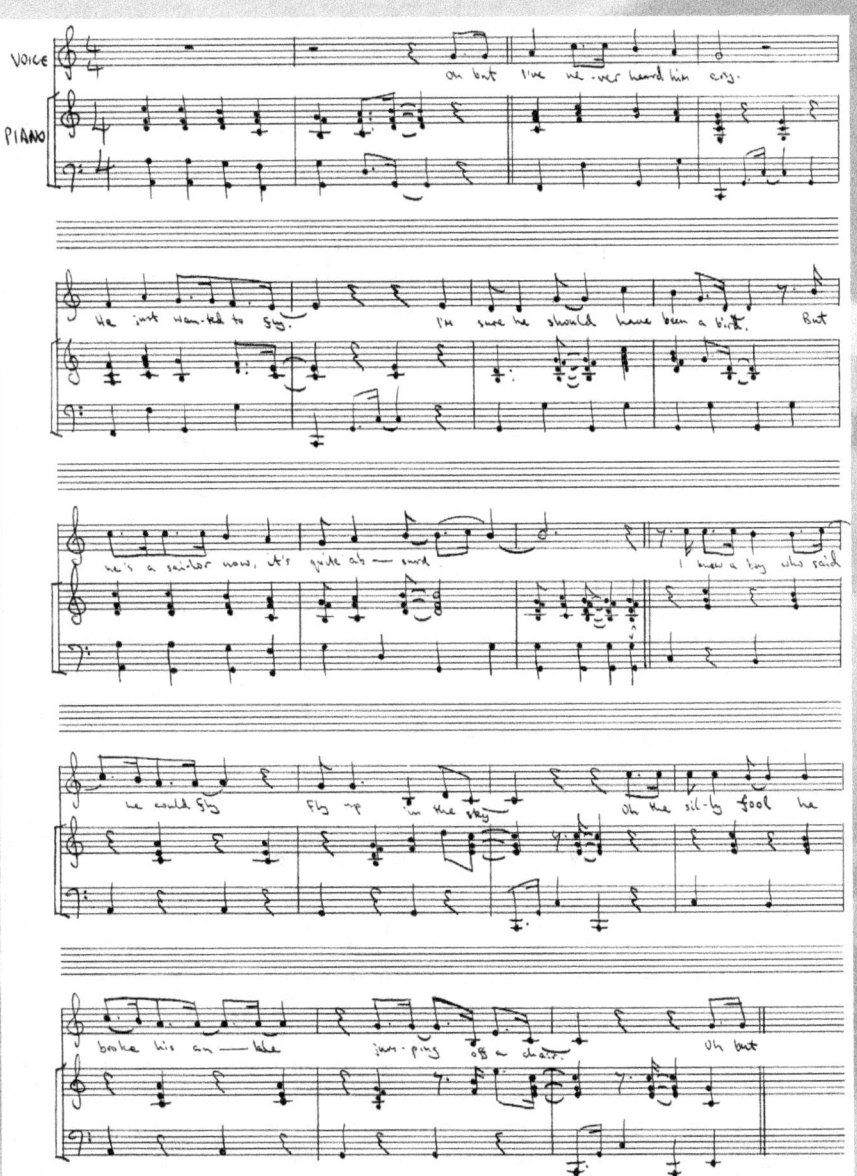

Chewee Chewee Chewing Gum

C   F   C
If Junes the month of roses if Junes the time of year

they'll be pollen up our noses

     F   G7
and sneezing in the air

   F   C
for the flowers are kissing one another

   F   C
with the help of the bees and the breezes

   F   C
it means we'll be covered everywhere

G7
everywhere with sneezes

F   C   F   C
achewachewacheweecheew

I Became What I Wanted To Be

trains coming round the bend
they'll be trains going over the rails
trains that are for sale
trains going up and down the trails
CHOoCHOoCHOoCHOoCHOo

chewee chewe chewing gum
there'll be chewing gum
on the back of the stair case
chewing gum on the back of the chair
chewing gum all over your hair
yumyumyumyummyyumyum

owls in the middle of the night
they'll be owls flying over the hay stacks
owls that can hoot in flight
owls that can make you frightened
OoOoOoOoOo

PRS for Music Tune Code 323654CS ISWC: T-011.367.863-9

Hedgehogs

  F#m   C#m
Down the Road round the corner
  F#m   C#m
is a tumbled down old house
  Bm   Em
it's got a dark ghostly garden
F (no bar)   E
someone strange lives inside my brother said

there are slugs in the garden

spiders and wood lice too

and when no body is looking they cheep into the house too

       A   B7   E
oh but we've got Hedgehogs in our garden
       A   B7   E
and they grow there very very well
       A   B7   E
they eat all the slugs and chase the spiders
B7   E
and that's how the little Hedgehogs grow

down the Road round the corner
ils a tumbled down old house
it's got a dark ghostly garden
someone strange lives inside my brother said
there are slugs in the garden
spiders and wood lice too

and when no body is looking they cheep into your bed
and your bedroom too

oh but we've got Hedgehogs in our garden
and they grow there very very well
and we feed them some dog food each evening
and that's how the little Hedgehogs grow

PRS for Music Tune Code 323654EN

Hong Kong Monsoon

  A   E
We came to Hong Kong in the rainy season
D   A
we almost got drowned

the high wind was howling
   E   E
the high wind was howling
D   A
all around all around
D   A
all around all around

we don't know how the plane landed

in that storm

the pilot said he hadn't planned

to worry us all to worry us all

    D   E
flashing crashing
    D   E
thunder flashing
    D
rushing gushing

hurricane

PRS for Music Tune Code 323654EW ISWC: T-320.194.308-6

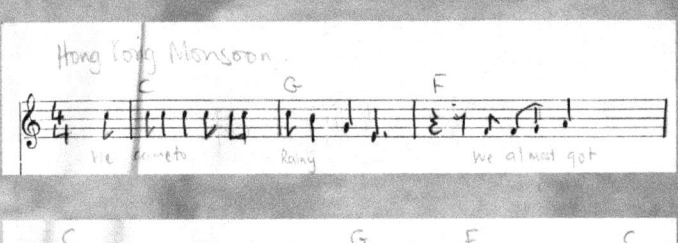
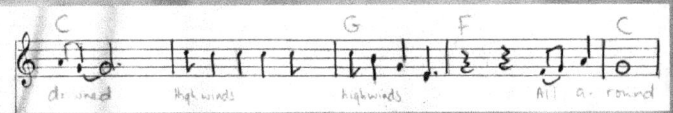

Hong Kong

Jungles of Borneo

(Single Note) d   c#   b   Em
Who killed the buffalo on the old Mura Road
(Single Note) d   c#   b   Em
who killed the buffalo on the old Mura Road

      Em   G   Em
jungle gongs in the dead of night
      Em   G Em
cicadas buzz mosquitoes bite

      Em   G   Em
horn bills fly they screech in flight

(E Shape no Bar) G   F#   F   Em
out in the jungles of Borneo

(E Shape no Bar) G   F#   F   Em
out in the jungles of Borneo

Em	G

long House the Iban's rise

| Em | G |

in former days they'd split your eyes

| Em | G |

with blow pipe your head they'd rise

sweat dripping in the shade

tatoos hidden in the glade

orang-utan's hide and babies cry

PRS for Music Tune Code 323654ER ISWC: T-320.194.302-0

Labi Jungle Brunei

Christmas Night

E7 D7 C7 B7 E   E7 D7 C7 B7 E

(use B7 shape on 6th 4th 3rd fret)*

Bludali Buddali Bum

E7 D7 C7 B7 E
Bludali Buddali Bum

E
 I woke up on a Christmas night

I saw a man dressed in red and white
A
I said Hey what you doing in here

you're not a relative
E
you're a stranger with a bard
B7
my Mum and Dad told me to shout NO
A
but you're a funny looking man and your covered in snow

E7 D7 C7 B7 E   (use B7 shape on 6th 4th 3rd fret)
*Bludali Buddali Bum
E7 D7 C7 B7 E
Bludali Buddali Bum

he said don't you recognise me
you see my face by every Christmas Tree
I said oh yes you are the famous politician
he said no I'm not and I'm the other one either

he said you have written to me
asking for lots of presents
now let me see
a super bike and a music player
and a super Sony Special games player

I said Hey you're a real cool dude
so you're Father Christmas and you are really true
he walked to the chimney
picked up his sack
he started to climb up into the black
I said Hey thanks He shouted back
that's ok have a good one back

well I ripped of the wrappers and I got stuck in
It was then to my horror the problems begin
For that Sony was a Micro-Soft player
I shouted out the window
hey you with the bard come back here
you've given me the wrong gear

well Father Christmas looked back at me
he said be kind be gracious
and next year we'll see
but for now all the boxes are empty
and the next time you write don't forget to say please
and next time don't you call me dude
from now on I'm Father Christmas to you

Rattattattooee

     C   G7   F   C
We climbed the stair to see granddad's hair
       G7   F C
because granddad's hair made us stare

         G7   F   C
it was a cloud of silver white and it seemed so very bright
                     G7   C
just like he'd had a fright in the middle of the night
      F   C   F   C
* Rattattattooee rattattattooee
   F   G7   C
rattattattooee vinderloo oo oo ee

bathing with your clothes on
washing your teeth with bleach
sometimes you were so crazy you just seemed out of reach
digging your vegetables or in the sea off Mombassa beech

*

you're on your train and you steamed away
I just hope it was like in the good old days
the Great Western from Tottness or Torquay
the next time you're passing whistle one for me

*

Written about 1979

King Kudwig

Em
King Ludwig was a mad man

so they say a a a a
Am   Em
he built castles in Bavaria anyway
Bm
he loved Wagner's Opera
Am   Gm   F#m
and didn't want to fight the Prussian Wars
G   D
*but Ludwig loved the Swans
C   G
white see how they shine
C   G   D
drifting on the waters of the woods of
G
Nueschawstein

His friend Bismarck
was the ruler of many land a a ands
but he couldn't save Ludwig from the work of idle hands
the politicians Lied Ludwig took the blame
they laughed and they called him insane

*

Whit Sunday 1886
Ludwig went walking with his doctor
but he was not sick
some how he drowned in the Lake
strange know one knows quite how

PRS for Music Tune Code 323654FN ISWC: T-320.194.312-2

By Unknown author - alexander palace forums, Public Domain,
https://commons.wikimedia.org/w/index.php?curid=8380182

Rainbows

        C
Rainbows rainbows
   F   C
coming out in different colours
C   F   C
water water rushes and gushes down the nullers
            G7
flowers start growing and I get going

C   Em   Am   G7   F   G7   C
red orange yellow green blue indigo violate
C   Em   Am   G7   F   G7   C
red orange yellow green blue indigo violate

        C
rainbows rainbows
   F   C
coming out in different colours
C   F   C
water wWater rushes and gushes down the nullers

        G7
we'll find some gold and share it between us
        C
for when were old
        G7
and when that day comes

we'll climb to the

I Became What I Wanted To Be

215

```
C      Em    Am    G7     F    G7    C
red orange yellow green blue indigo violate
C      Em    Am    G7     F    G7    C
red orange yellow green blue indigo violat
              F              C
    we'll say Rainbow you are our Hero
           G7                    C
    and we thank you for giving us your gold
           G7                    C
    we'll say rainbow you are our hero
                    G7
    and we thank you for giving us your

C      Em    Am    G7     F    G7    C
red orange yellow green blue indigo violate
C      Em    Am    G7     F    G7    C
red orange yellow green blue indigo violate
```

PRS for Music Tune Code 323654DS ISWC: T-320.194.295-8
Lyrics from a poem by Alexine Courtney 1981

Rainbows

Rainbows come out in different
colours,
Water rushes and gushes down the
nullahs,
The flowers start growing,
The wind starts blowing,
The water starts flowing,
And keeps going.
If you and I,
Float up to the sky,
We'll slide down the rainbow,
We'll find some gold,
We'll share it between us for when
we are old,
Then I'll go to the rainbow,
And say you're my hero,
For giving us some of your gold.

Alexcine Courtney
Aged 8 years
Kennedy Road Junior School

I Became What I Wanted To Be   217

The Berlin Zoo Song

```
C                                    F
I had a lovely day at the zoo with you today
   G7                           C
   five bucks wasn't that much to pay
                                F
   we saw a lion a tiger and a kangaroo
           G7              C
   saw a Berliner bear and a baby Gnu

            F
   *when we went to the zoo
         C
   oh when we went to the zoo
   G7                           C
   when we went to the zoo today
F                     C
we got off the bus there was a Duck-Bill-Platypus
   G7                         C
   when we went to the zoo today


   C                             F
   the keeper looked like mw the monkeys looked like you
      G7                           C
   hanging around their cages was all they could do
                                  F
   the Sea Lions ball hit you right on the nose
                 G7         C
and the baboons red bottom glowed as he picked at his toes

                 *
         F                          C
   we saw a giraffe the polar bears made us laugh
         G7
   when we went to the Zoo today
```

PRS for Music Tune Code 323654CN ISWC: T-011.367.790-9 Written 1982

Water

    C
Swim swim swimming pool
         G7
makes you nice nice and cool
   C
bath bath bathing in a tub
  G7   C
it's so nice to have a scrub
F
the water goes swush the water goes wush
                     C
the water goes up your nose
G7
you need water to drink and water to sink
                C
and water to wash your clothes

crocodiles crocodiles

in your bath aren't much fun

you'd better watch out you'd better watch out

or they'll bite your bottom

crocodiles crocodiles

in you tea cup aren't much fun

you'd better watch out you'd better watch out

or they'll eat your current bun

fountains fountains

spraying high the water can hit you in the eye

hoses hoses watering roses

rain coming from the sky

PRS for Music Tune Code 323654DV ISWC: T-320.194.298-1

Afton Water Scotland

The Swedish Reindeer Song

  Am
Mind you said the boy with the blond hair
     G
   we've been around the world
  F
 seen diamond rings and carpet shops
    E7
   cafes and strings of pearls

   F   G
*and where are we today Ianto
   A   B   B A# A
 not Denmark Hong Kong
  F   G
and where will we be tomorrow Ianto
    A   B   B A# A
 not Denmark Hong Kong

I Became What I Wanted To Be

mind you said the mouse from America

we've seen some mighty fine things

seen the sun shine above the rain

across the aeroplanes wings

*

mind you said the Monkey with the red cap

we've been around the world

from the tropics of South East Asia

to the chills of Oslo

*

mind you said the daddy with the little hair

we've been around the world

The Policeman's Find

     Am   Am
What's this I've found the policeman said
  G   G
in the middle of the night and in this bed
     F   F
his hair was white and his teeth were red
E7   E7
with the policeman's torch shining on his head

it's only me he said rolling on the floor
trying to climb over to the door
it's back was small it's bottom was small
the policeman said stand still all

please don't it said I'm only small
and look at you your 6 feet tall
my lips are green my neck is too
and look at you you're all dressed in blue

alright said the policeman I'll let you go
but don't go suddenly go very slow
with your ears of green and your toes of yellow
I remember you now you're that fellow

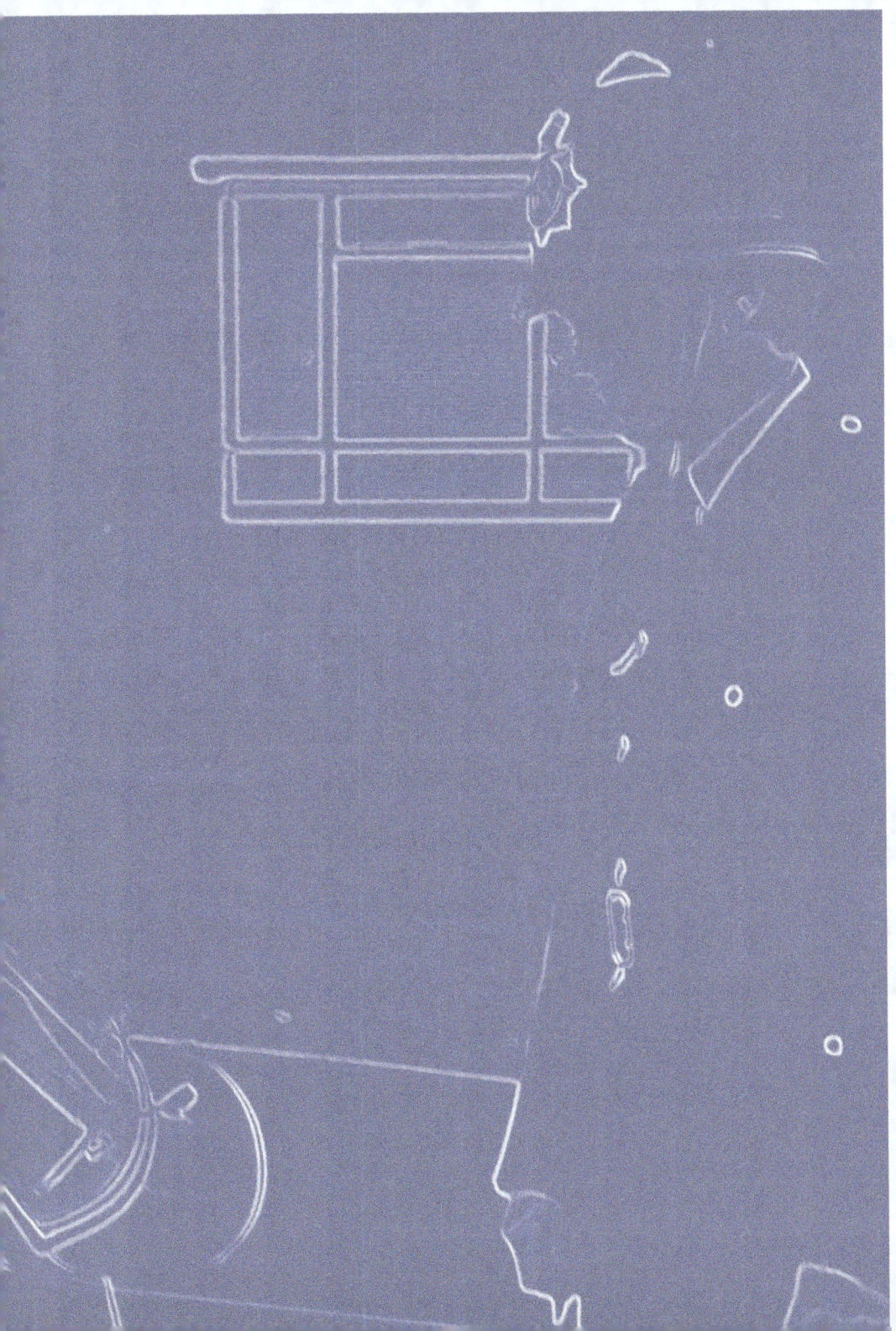

The Portuguese

       Am   G
It was the Portuguese who had dirty knees
      F   E7   Am
when they knelt down in the mud
Am   G   F   E7   Am
and the Indian Scared Cow was always chewing at the cud
             C   E7
but the Americans they were the ones
      Am   E7
who came with such a thud
Am   E7   Am   E7   Am
if the Martians come to earth will they bring their own soap
      suds
     C   E7
goodness gracious me
   Am   E7
goodness gracious me
   Am   E7   Am
goodness gracious me

I Became What I Wanted To Be

now the French they eat frogs legs
and they eat lots of snails
and the Belgium's bring their children up
on French fries and finger nails
and the Japanese some times have dirty knees
and they eat steaks of whale
if we all lived on the moon and ate sheep's eyes
would we go to jail

now the Italians built a tower leaning to one side
now the Russians built a Kremlin to keep their politicians in
but the Australians have kangaroos
and they have wallabies
if a koala bear sat on your lap
would his flees tickle your knees

PRS for Music Tune Code 323654DR ISWC: T-320.194.294-7

His Gazoo

```
         G                         C
It was a stormy night when the elves took flight
           D                    G
      and the bees went on honeymoon
   C        D        G          C
the wind so strong we could not hear the song
                       D         G
        of the little boy and his gazoo


           G          C   D
      *Oh it was his gazoo ooo
                   G
        that went la da da da da
                      C    D
         oh it was his gazoo ooo
                   G
        that went oo oo oo oo oo


                    G              C
  the waves were high and the boat was tossed
              D                G
        the captain cried to his god
   G                             C
  he said my lord I'd think that all was lost
            D                     G
    but I can still hear my sons  gazoo
```

I Became What I Wanted To Be

that god looked down upon the frightened man
he held out his loving hand
he plucked the sailor from beneath the wave
he said for your son you will be saved

the sailor came home the very next day
he said to his son come on over here and play
play me a tune upon your toy
for my life has been saved for you my boy

PRS for Music Tune Code 323654DN ISWC: T-320.194.292-5 Written 1977

Lewis Cedar

Up in the Clouds

```
     C                        F
I Was up in the clouds in the sky
     C
 when I saw a cow flying by
        G7                   C
she said it's hard to make a living these days
          F             C
    and this is the only way
      F                      G7
to keep up with you jet setting people
```

I was driving in a friends Rolls Royce
when up Galloped a horse called Boyce
he said you know I have run all this way
I forgotten completely what I was going to say
give me a ride and I'll try to remember

I was sailing on a millionaires yacht
when onto the Bridge a Pig did trot
he said I'm here to encourage vegetarianism
your galley space is just like a prison
my piglets photo will make your chef cry

PRS for Music Tune Code 323654DU ISWC: T-320.194.301-9

Ozone Layer

```
        A                    E         A
We were running to the piste when it rained
         G                          G
   it was that no snow syndrome again
       F                        G
   fog hung heavy round the mountain side
              A         B
      a scientist in a micro light cried

 B  A# A       A  G#   C                C
         ozone ozone layer
               A  G#      C
         ozone ozone layer


            A                      A
       just then I tripped over in the snow
            G                       G
       my skis were buckled and I hurt my toe
          F                             F
      the snow was icy my ski poles were bent
       G                          A       B
   and all the children laughed it wasn't pleasant


 B  A# A        A  G#    C                C
          Ha Ha Ha Ha Ha Ha
                A  G#       C
          Ha Ha Ha Ha Ha Ha
```

I'd tripped on a tuft of grass
and as we stared in turned into a bath
hot springs were trickling from the mountainside
a conservationist in a cable car cried
ozone ozone layer
ozone ozone layer

we were running to the piste when it rained
it was that no snow syndrome again
hot springs were trickling from the mountainside
a conservationist and the Scientist cried

ozone ozone layer
ozone ozone layer

just then a boat from Africa came by
with a sign say water skis for hire
he said hey man I like your ski suit
but come on baby can you water shoot

Ha Ha Ha Ha Ha Ha
Ha Ha Ha Ha Ha Ha

we were running to the piste when it rained
it was that no snow syndrome again
hot springs were trickling from the mountainside
a conservationist and the scientist cried

ozone Ha Ha Ha
ozone Ha Ha HA hhhhhhhhhh

Did You Ever Have A Dream

    Am
      I was in a small fishing boat
Em
      in the middle of the Sea
    F   D7
when suddenly a sea lion climbed in
      G7   E7
      and started kissing me

    F   C
    *did you ever have a dream ?
G7   C
    did you ever have a dream ?
  F   C
    did you ever have a dream
          G7
    that was real ?

I was in a helicopter
it had a seat like a children's swing
the fuel was Pepsi Cola
in a Pepsi Cola tin

*

I was driving with my daddy
along the motorway
when suddenly he fainted
I grabbed the wheel and I saved the day

I Became What I Wanted To Be

*

  C
I've dreamed about my mummy
  F
and I've dreamed about my dad
  G7
I've dreamed about my girl friend
  C
but I'm not going to tell you about that
E7   Am
except she kisses better than the sea lion

*

I was on a ladder
a hundred feet up in the air
when suddenly the ladder toppled over
and I was flying through the air

MCPS/PRS Tune Code 323493ET ISWC: T-011.458.310-6

A Set of Magic Tricks

    G   C
They gave me a box of Lego bricks
        G   C
and a set of magic tricks
    G   C
my teachers said we are done
    G   C
time to hit the world have some fun

    Am   Am
there were some cold streets
    Em   Em
many dark alleys

 F   C
three girls I remember one whose name was Sally
  Am   Am
all of a sudden ten years had gone by
   Em   Em
I was in the public eye
F   C
poster all about the town Leslie Crowther said come on down

I Became What I Wanted To Be

*

     Am   Am
I did TV for plenty of money
    Em   Em
Frank Spencer was very funny
Am   Am
with guitar and puppets I travelled over the seas
   F   C
in twenty five lands they welcomed me

*

     Am   Am
young and old all colours creeds
    Em   Em
those wonderful people
F   C
helped me succeed so my life has been free

Finished 14 11 2022

What I Want To Be

C   C
Hear the coin jingle in my pocket
F   C
feel the note rustle in my hand
F   C
all pound notes and fivers
G7   C
with this I can demand

C   C
*but I tell you I'd give all of it
F   F
and a hundred times more
G7   G
if I could be what I want to be
                        C
and nothing more

I've seen Fort Knox on the TV
I watched the gold yellow bars
with my feet on the settee
I stared really hard

*

I've got my cheque book handy
got some money in the bank
got an account on deposit
and some money in the savings
bank

*

Written 16 October 1974

Lewis Cedar

I Became What I Wanted To Be

Many thanks for my career

John Spencer, John Phipps, Tom Paxton, Henry Edwards,
Arthur Stacey, Mr Keening, Geoffrey Smith, Ted Bloomfield,
Doug Pie, Mr Mulhern, Barry Stimpson, Mervin Hall,
Roger and Sandra Butler, Ray Figg, Bob Kember,
Richard James, Barry Vines,
Mike Robertson, Mike Watson, Marianne Segal, Dave Waite,
Ken, Con, Pat, Peewee, Andy Bennett, Jack Firestein,
Nigel Cameron, Mark and Tricia Smith, Theo Johnson,
Martin and Janette Orkin, Johnny Spillers, Al Lee,
Eddie Francis, Len Tucker, Norman Newell, Len Marten,
Doris Barry, Adrian Towler, David Hartley,
Shayne Render, Marion Parks, Jean Grant,
Donald Sibitzki, Alan Sudron, Richard Whitehouse,
Michael Bennett, Rob Ashmore, Elizabeth Anson,
Tony Banes, Vaughan Savage, Nick Bailey, Adrian Love,
Tommy Vance, Robert Mulvey, Toby Coghill,
David Bedford, Cheryl Campbell, Melvin Hayes,
Marjatta and Roland Fuelleman, Urs Kneubuehl
Ralph Kradolfer, Marc Ellington, John Duncanson.
Family members and
all who provided me with shows
and hospitality, kindness and understanding.

This list is not complete by any means

Lewis Cedar

No:	Song Title	Page	PRS Tune Code	Written
1	Elm Fires	16	323492LQ	1974
2	Marvellous Restaurant	17	323492LT	08 Jun 1973
3	Hotel in Germany	18	323492LS	06 Sep 1978
4	Old Grey Coat	22	323492LU	24 Apr 1973
5	Photographs	24	323492LV	01 Apr 1979
6/7	I'd Love To Know	27	323492LR	10 Sep 1978
8	Tavernelle	28	323492LW	1979
9	Lovely Weather	30	323493AP	23 April 1974
10	Maybe If I Want Too	31	323493AN	01 July 1974
11	I Wish You Had Have Come Along	32	323493AM	1979
12	Your New Song	34	323493AR	18 May 1975
13	Just Nice Words	36	323493AQ	12 Dec 1971
14	Spanish Dancer	37	323493BN	1986
15	What Do You Do In Holland	38	323493AS	1981
16	Nairobi	40	323493AT	1981
17	Mombassa	42	323493AU	1981
18	Across The South China Sea	44	323493AV	1983
19	Experience	47	323493CP	1973
20	Kalamansi	48	323493AW	1983
21	What About Our Baby	49	323493BP	1986

I Became What I Wanted To Be

No:	Song Title	Page	PRS Tune Code	Written
22	I Brought You To The Alpine Mountains	50	323493BM	1986
23	Peter Pan Summer	52	323493BQ	1988
24	Victory is Ours	54	323493BR	1982
25	Just To Survive	57	323493BS	1978
25	Back In The States	58	323493CR	1990
27	If I Had Done Something Else	60	323493CS	1992
28	What Did Mrs Beatie Do ?	63	323493CT	1982
29	Lean On Me Any Time That You Want Too	66	323493CW	Feb 1995
30	Juke Box Baby	68	323493CU	18 Mar 1976
31	Anke's Song	70	323493BT	1990
32	Nigel's Song	72	323493BU	1992
33	We Went To Vienna	74	323493BV	1990
34	Sweet Years	77	323493CV	1975
35	He Gave Her The Frangipani	78	323493BW	1988
36	Richmond Lullaby	81	323493DM	1972
37	Hangs Together	82	323493CM	1973
38	When The Lady Says Good Bye	84	323493CN	1990
39	When I Was Your Age	86	323493CQ	1991
40	I Could Say That I Miss Annie	88	323493DN	1981
41	My Passport Says Planet Earth	90	323493DP	1993

No:	Song Title	Page	PRS Tune Code	Written
42	Mister Producer Make Me A Star	92	323493DQ	01 Jan 1975
43	As Far As Hong Kong	94		1992
44	Land of the Filipino	98	323493DR	1986
45/46	Did You Hear the Spanish Lady	100	323493DS	1988
47	She Powers What I Can Be	102	323493DT	15 Feb 2005
48	Dream Dream Dream	103	323493ES	
49	I Hope The Years and You Have Been Good Together	104	323493DU	Jul 2005
50	I'm the Boy who Played Tom Paxton's Guitar	106	323493DV	Feb 2005
51	Time To Start Out On Your Own	108	323493DW	2004
52	I Was Born and I Was Born Here	110	323493EM	2006
53	Christine's Smiling like the Sun in June	113	323493EN	2006
54	The Gift To Be Free	114	323493EP	2006
55	Mrs Beckham	116	323493EQ	2006
56	Ching Chong China Man	119	323493EU	
57	Oo Char Tra La La	120	323493ER	
58	Game Boy	122	323493FM	
59	Bananas	124	323493EW	
60	I Can	126	323493FN	
61	It's Funny How People Can Be	128	323493EV	
62	Uncle Percy	130	323493FP	

I Became What I Wanted To Be

No:	Song Title	Page	PRS Tune Code	Written
63	Did You Hear About The Man Who Lost His Trousers	132	323493FQ	
64	Time	134	323493FR	
65	Plus est en Vous— More is In You	136	323493FS	Mar 1993
66	It's Just the Being With You	144	323654FT	July 2007
67	When I'm 63	146		2020
68	Relax Baby Life's a Choice	148	323493FT	Feb 2007
69	Rapunzel Let Down Your Hair	150	323654FS	Feb 2007
70	Say You Can	152	323493FU	
71	Councillor Chedwiggen	154		22 Oct 1974
72	I Hope You Will Remember This Song	155	323654GQ	19 Mar 2008
73	Enjoy the Itch Don't Scratch It	156		15 Mar 2009
74	Oh You Have A Lovely Voice	158	323654GP	Feb 2008
75	If You Thought that the Rails Were Forever	160	323654GS	31 Jul 1973
76	Hey Holly	162	323654FV	Nov 1996 to Aug 22 2007
77	Fight the Tide	163	323654FW	Aug 2007
78	Marry Me	164	323654GM	Aug 1976
79	May Your Life be an Apple Crumble	165		
80	Three Pretty Ladies	166	323654GT	Mar 2008 Jun 2009
81	Super Sea Morning	168		31 Jan 1974
82/83	The Forth Bridge Song	170	323654GR	4 Aug 1974

No:	Song Title	Page	PRS Tune Code	Written
84	Sing It One More Time Again	172		9 Feb 9 Mar 2009
85	Knight At You're Round Table	174		Feb Jun 2009
86	The Highway Man	176		1972
87	I Say You're Beautiful	178	323654FU	29 Aug 2007 7 Sep 2007
88	The Traveller	180		2020
89	Man With One Shoe	182	323653AQ	2016
90	Routes De Soleil	185	323654DT	
91	King Fisher	186		Spring 2020
92	Pyjama Game	188	323654GN	Mar 2005
93	Bad Boy	189	323654CP	1989
94	Chain of Freedom	190		Aug 2007
95	Chocolate Milk	192	323654FQ	1985
96	Elephant Parrot and Kangaroo	194	323654CT	
97	Granddad's Car Horn	197	323654CV	
98	Go To Singapore	198	323654CU	
99	He Just Wanted to Fly	200	323654DM	
100	Chewee Chewee Chewing Gum	202	323654CS	
101	Hedgehogs	204	323654EN	

I Became What I Wanted To Be

No:	Song Title		PRS Tune Code	Written
102	Hong Kong Monsoon	206	323654EW	
103	Jungles of Borneo	208	323654ER	
104	Christmas Night	210		
105	Rattattattooee	212		
106	King Ludwig	213	323654FN	
107	Rainbows	216	323654DS	
108	The Berlin Zoo Song	217	323654CN	1982
109	Water	218	323654DV	
110	The Swedish Reindeer Song	220	323654EU	
111	The Policeman's Find	222	323654FP	
112	The Portuguese	224	323654DR	
113	His Gazoo	226	323654DN	1977
114	Up in the Clouds in the Sky	229	323654DU	
115	Ozone Layer	230	323654EV	
116	Did You Ever Have A Dream	232	323493ET	
117	A Set of Magic Tricks	234		2023
118	If I Could Be What I Want To Be	236		16 Oct 1974

Picture Credits

Elm Tress
By Kim Traynor - Own work, CC BY-SA 3.0, https://commons.wikimedia.org/w/index.php?curid=17372763

Tommy Vance
By Ssaco - Own work, CC BY-SA 3.0, https://commons.wikimedia.org/w/index.php?curid=16436642

Kalamansi
By Obsidian Soul - Own work, CC0, https://commons.wikimedia.org/w/index.php?curid=81931708

Peter Pan
By Francis Donkin Bedford - Illustration from "Peter and Wendy" by James Matthew Barrie, Published 1911 by C. Scribner's Sons, New York, Public Domain, https://commons.wikimedia.org/w/index.php?curid=147924058

Juke Box
By Frederic Pasteleurs - Own work, CC BY-SA 3.0, https://commons.wikimedia.org/w/index.phpcurid=861509

Frangipanni
By Varun Pabrai - Own work, CC BY-SA 4.0, https://commons.wikimedia.org/w/index.php?curid=45012377

John Glenn
By NASA - NASA Commons on Flickr, Public Domain, https://commons.wikimedia.org/w/index.php?curid=75150

Yuri Gagarin
By Arto Jousi / /Suomen valokuvataiteen museo / Alma Media / Uuden Suomen kokoelma; Restored by Adam Cuerden - Finnish Museum of Photography, Public Domain, https://commons.wikimedia.org/w/index.php?curid=79901445

The Earth NASA

Francisco Franco
By Unknown author - Biblioteca Virtual de Defensa: RETRATO DEL GRAL. FRANCISCO FRANCO BAHAMONDE (MUE-120973), CC0, https://commons.wikimedia.org/w/index.php?curid=70812173

Game Boy
By Evan-Amos - Own work, Public Domain, https://commons.wikimedia.org/w/index.php?curid=36853230

Bananas
By Steve Hopson, www.stevehopson.com, CC BY-SA 2.5, https://commons.wikimedia.org/w/index.php?curid=1541726

Wilma Rudolf
By Lindeboom, Henk / Anefo - [1] Dutch National Archives, The Hague, Fotocollectie Algemeen Nederlands Persbureau (ANEFO), 1945-1989, Nummer toegang 2.24.01.03 Bestanddeelnummer 911-6074, CC BY-SA 3.0 nl, https://commons.wikimedia.org/w/index.php?curid=29651399

Wilma Rudolf Running
By The original uploader was Kasper2006 at Italian Wikipedia. - Uploaded from it.wikipedia.org, Public Domain, https://commons.wikimedia.org/w/index.php?curid=22115160

Rapunzel
By Paul Hey - https://www.childstories.org/vi/rapunzen-1832.html, Public Domain, https://commons.wikimedia.org/w/index.php?curid=98274134

Knights Round Table
By Evrard d'Espinques -Gallica, Public Domain, https://commons.wikimedia.org/w/index.phpcurid=24915213

Christmas Tree
A Clarke

Ludwig II
By Unknown author - alexander palace forums, Public Domain, https://commons.wikimedia.org/w/index.php?curid=8380182

Ozone Layer
By Earth Science and Remote Sensing Unit, Lyndon B. Johnson Space Center - JSC Gateway to Astronaut Photography of Earth, Public Domain, https://commons.wikimedia.org/w/index.php?curid=108456866

Others https://www.spvr.org

Some of the music staves John Spencer